Working with
Anxious, Nervous, and
Depressed Children

A Spiritual Perspective to Guide Parents

Working with Anxious, Nervous, and Depressed Children

A Spiritual Perspective to Guide Parents

by
Henning Köhler

Introduction by
Philip Incao, MD

Waldorf
PUBLICATIONS

Published by:
Waldorf Publications
Research Institute for Waldorf Education
38 Main Street
Chatham, New York 12037

Title: *Working with Anxious, Nervous, and Depressed Children*
A Spiritual Perspective to Guide Parents

Original Title: *Von Ängstlichen Traurigen und Unruhigen Kindern*
Grundlagen einer spirituellen Erziehungspraxis
1995, ISBN 3-7725-1186-4

Originally published by: Verlag Freies Geistesleben

Author: Henning Köhler
Translated by: Marjorie Spock
Medical Consultant: Philip Incao, MD
Editor: David Mitchell
Proofreaders: Nancy Jane, Katarina Noyes, Judy Grumstrup-Scott

ISBN 1-978-888365-28-3

Table of Contents

Editorial Comments

New spiritually based solutions in parenting and in education are needed to heal some of the complex problems we are observing in our modern children.

While contemporary psychologists turn to allopathic drugs and invent new classifications to label troubled children, Henning Köhler comes forth courageously to put forward his thoughts based on a spiritual foundation for healing.

His direction is grounded in an understanding of how the senses are awakened and how the social community of the family can be strengthened.

Henning Köhler (born in 1951) is well known and appreciated throughout Europe for his work as a therapeutic educator. He has written several books and given numerous lectures concerning questions on education. He founded the Janusz-Korczak-Institute, near Stuttgart, Germany where he and his coworkers run a clinic for children and young people with educational or developmental problems.

We are appreciative that this valuable book is now available for the English-speaking world.

– David Mitchell
Editor
Boulder, Colorado
January 2001

Introduction

Philip Incao, M.D.

This is a remarkable and unusual book even within the category of works related to Rudolf Steiner. Its topic is eminently practical and timely: how to understand and address the increasingly prevalent difficulties and dysfunctions of today's children.

The author's approach is extremely refreshing in that he builds entirely on his experience as a therapist with such children, experience in which much thought, love, and enthusiasm have obviously been applied. This gives the book a liveliness and immediacy rarely found in educational writing today. One senses that the book's content has grown organically out of the author's years of practical work with children.

One senses also the author's powerful "will to heal," which is so much emphasized by Steiner as the only path to fruitful insights and interventions in therapeutic work.

This is an inspired, robust, and groundbreaking book. Like Alexander standing before the Gordian knot, Köhler cuts through the intricacies of modern materialistic theory of children's dysfunctions (by ignoring them) and very early in the book suggests to his readers a bold step: apply to your child's guardian angel for help!

> The term "angel" may disturb you. We could agree on a less bothersome one, though why do we need to? A strange modern embarrassment stands in the way of opening ourselves to imaginations; instead, we allow everything to be dragged down to the level of gray lifeless conceptualizing.

Abstract scientific terminology is particularly out of place in discussing children.

But please understand me: I am not using the term angel symbolically or metaphorically; I am completely serious, and beg you to take it literally. In speaking of imaginations, I'm not referring to fantasies, but to facts .... I'll take the liberty of simply asserting that to assume that angels exist can be very useful under certain circumstances, and that our practically oriented approach accords very well with such an assumption. We should put it to the test.

Henning Köhler reverses the usual order of things and comes to the remedy before discussing the diagnosis. The remedy is simple and profound and is worthwhile repeating here: parents, teachers, and therapists may receive the inspiration, insights, and attitudes needed to help a particular child if they follow certain steps of surrender and self-discipline. First,

... The ongoing practice of overcoming one's own habitual judgments, desires, expectations and concepts, pushing them out of the way and giving oneself instead to listening and observing in what might be called an ever marveling attentiveness to the child's image in the here and now, every least detail of which deserves your whole-hearted and unjudgmental interest .... When you begin to feel a kind of tenderness awakening in you for the child's very faults and weaknesses, for all the things that ordinarily lead to strife and anger, you will know that you are on the right path.

With this ongoing practice of selflessness as the indispensable basis for all healing work, Köhler then builds these further steps (inspired by Rudolf Steiner) in his practical method of appealing to a child's guardian angel for help before falling asleep at night:

1. Guidelines in the form of ideas are indeed a necessity! It is they which lead us to the image formed in meditative questioning and carried into sleep with us. To have concerned oneself with the anthroposophical background of children's developmental crises is not only advisable, but absolutely essential. But that is not enough, for it remains head knowledge, and we are at once confronted with the need to take a further step.

2. [Take into sleep] . . . a clearly thought-out problem that concerns you deeply for the child's sake rather than a problem of your own.

3. [Take into sleep] . . . a really clear image of the child . . . having taken the trouble to observe the child keenly and lovingly at least once a day . . . with reverence for the child.

4. What can be achieved in this way is naturally much richer, more and more deeply grounded, than any head knowledge one might try . . . to translate into action . . . mostly in vain. You experience how an insight, one that you are neither able nor willing to put into immediate practice but rather continue to meditate on as a questioning carried into sleep, works formatively, *reshaping the structure of your habits.* (emphasis mine) And you experience, too, how you are enabled to read the "answer" in your own changing conduct. It is an answer you could not have found by any amount of merely theoretical searching . . . . You are dealing here with a primal phenomenon that offers you a method that can be developed and built into a psychological tool . . . . We call upon a wisdom that lives deep within us, a wisdom not available to waking consciousness . . . . Finding answers by this method has to be based on genuine interest and involvement; we must really be stirred by a desire to understand the child's being.

How different is this approach from today's medical research! Köhler makes no concession to, no compromise with conventional scientific, materialistic thinking. You will find nothing on brain development in this book, simply because (if I read Köhler rightly) such knowledge is merely descriptive; it does not lead us to understand how to help the child in our care.

On the one hand, Steiner always emphasized that anthroposophic medicine and its allied therapies were not an alternative to, but rather a broadening of conventional medicine, the achievements of which he repeatedly praised. Conventional medicine and psychology are based on knowledge of the physical body and brain, which is certainly very important. Yet such knowledge is inevitably incomplete and apt to lead to false conclusions as long as the reality of the other three members of the human being—the spirit, soul, and life forces (etheric)—are left out of the healer's reckoning.

Thus, a four-dimensional human being is certainly broader than a one-dimensional human being. In this sense and this sense alone may anthroposophic medicine and therapies be considered a broadening or extension of conventional medicine.

When it comes to *understanding* the full reality of the human being and to *learning how to heal* based on this reality, then a mere broadening of conventional materialistic medical thinking will never suffice.

This is where the will to heal must come alive! As Steiner so strongly emphasized in his lectures to young doctors, without the will to heal, all medical knowledge is useless, because it does not lead to a true understanding of the human being.

This sounds strange and incredible to the modern mind. We are tempted to ask, "Why can't I pursue and discover knowledge for its own sake without necessarily willing to do something with it? Doesn't such willing come *after* I acquire the knowledge? How could the presence or absence of my will to do something with the knowledge affect the truthfulness of the knowledge itself?"

Steiner answers:

The feeling that we have about knowledge in all domains of life should lead to *reality*, not to formalism . . . .

In the mysteries, knowledge was inevitably withheld from those who merely desired it in the formal sense and [was] imparted only to those who had the will to lead over this knowledge into reality . . . . For a knowledge that is real cannot separate itself from the will—that is quite impossible.

Again, how different this is from the method of modern scientific research! Modern science is based on the assumption that human thinking and ingenuity alone are capable of discovering the deeper truth of things. According to Steiner, without right feeling and right willing, the most brilliant powers of thought will only lead to illusion and deception, not to reality and never to healing.

The method set forth here by Henning Köhler makes this quite clear right from the start. In his foreword to the book Köhler states ". . . those who hold that love has nothing to offer scientific thinking will scarcely gain much from this book . . ." By "love", Köhler of course means much more than kindness and sympathy. These are basic prerequisites for anyone starting out in therapeutic work, but are not powerful enough to reach the desired goal of healing. No, Köhler is talking about love as the irresistible, unquenchable fire of the spirit itself, as in Rudolf Steiner's verse "Victorious Spirit."

> Victorious Spirit
> Flame through the impotence
> Of irresolute souls,
> Burn out the egoism,
> Ignite the compassion,
> That selflessness
> The life stream of humankind
> Wells up as the source of spirit rebirth.

The love which is so indispensable for the pursuit of science and of healing is a reverent and selfless *devotedness of will*.

Anyone embarking on the path of scientific inquiry sooner or later finds himself or herself facing an inner test consciously or unconsciously, a questioning by the spirit standing guard over truth that goes something like this: "What are your motives in seeking this knowledge? Are they truly selfless? Are you willing to wait until you are mature enough to receive and bear this knowledge in a spirit of utter selflessness and to offer it in service to the world?"

Most medical researchers or healers today would not be equal to such a test.

This book suggests that Köhler is an exception to this statement. His proposed method for learning how to help today's difficult children is nothing less than a simple but profound path of schooling our thinking, heart, and will in selfless devotion to the child's destiny.

I am moved to comment on one further aspect of this book, the main content of which is a very illuminating treatise on the senses of life, touch, movement, and balance. Köhler shows how a disturbance of each sense may lead to a specific dysfunctional behavior—a disturbed life sense may lead to restlessness and hyperactivity, a disturbed touch sense to hypersensitivity and anxiety, and a disturbed movement sense to depressed, brooding behavior.

In his discussion of restless, hyperactive children Köhler states, "more and more children lean in this direction for reasons that cannot be further discussed here." This tantalizing statement begs to be followed up!

Indeed, what are the causes responsible for the growing epidemic of "attention deficit hyperactivity disorder" today in the United States and other postmodern countries? Much light needs to be shed on this subject. Perhaps Henning Köhler has discussed it already, or will do so in the future, in another book to be translated into English. But Köhler already hints at the reasons for the alarming increase in restless, hyperactive children today in two of this book's early chapters which merit the reader's special attention. These are: "Is the body too chilly for the soul?" and "A cool head and a warm heart." A full discussion of this topic would fill more than one book and is most urgently needed if we hope to arrest and eventually to reverse the dangerous deterioration today in both the bodily and soul health of our children.

Köhler makes clear the fundamental importance of *warmth* and hints at its special function in healthy child development. The warmth of love, caring, and compassion are received by the child's open heart and, if it is properly cared for, can flow in two directions: upward to warm the thinking with lively imagination and creativity and downward to warm the will in enthusiastic service to the world. Warmth is the magical element which corresponds to the living spirit itself and which is indispensable not only for the harmonious interworking of body, soul, and spirit, but also for the healthy unfolding of the child's willing, feeling, and thinking.

Everything in modern life that excessively or inappropriately cools down the inner warmth of the body or soul works against the child's own spirit, impeding its incarnation and the unfolding of its destiny. The continuing decrease in IQ of American youth accompanied by the almost fourfold increase in disability due to chronic physical and mental conditions in children since 1960 suggest to me that the spirit's warmth is being increasingly and dangerously thwarted in our society.

Our children are like the canaries in the coal mine; their dysfunction is a measure of the spiritual imbalance of our society. It is now the task of all of us, whether parent, teacher, or healer, to discern just where the healthy balance lies between warmth and coolness in both body and soul in each child in our care. The balance point will, of course, be different in each individual child and at different ages. The required discernment of the right balance in each case is not possible without an understanding of child development, health, and illness, based on spiritual science. It would seem that our society is very far from achieving such an understanding, but outer appearances often belie the forces of change working deeply in human souls.

Our task is to keep working in our individual fields of endeavor, in Köhler's words "with courage born of insight" to build living, inspiring, and empowering bridges from anthroposophy to our own practical work, so that the healing so desperately needed today may flow into human life and into our struggling Earth. This book is a significant contribution to that healing work.

Foreword

This book is essentially a series of lectures I delivered and revised for printing. Although a certain amount of stylistic grooming and some supplementation seemed advisable, I have tried to keep its tone informal. A text of this nature can obviously not be compared with a written one, and anyone who is looking for a systematic structuring will not find it here; there is repetition, reviewing, and side commentary, typical of a spoken handling of the themes. I hope, however, that these faults will be made up for by the liveliness of the spoken word which still characterizes the printed pages. The book's theme itself calls for such a style, as readers will note.

The lecture material has been linked and supplemented, and then given chapter headings, making for a continuous, expanded text, whose theme is basal sense maturation. It is examined from the standpoint of anthroposophical developmental psychology, focusing particularly on establishing a topology of structuring child behavior on the basis of which immediate consequences for educational practice can be drawn.

Although I will be discussing these consequences, it is by no means my intention to supply pedagogical recipes. It will rather be apparent that I am seeking to encourage parents to do independent study and to strengthen their self-confidence in handling quite difficult situations. My happiest hours as a child therapist and educational consultant have been those in which I could bid parents good-bye with the words, "Now you don't need me anymore." A consultant's most important task is to work with parents to develop an understanding of the true nature of human beings.

The present volume offers insights on this score derived from research carried on over the years by the curative/pedagogical section of the Janusz-Korczak Institute, in both internal and public undertakings. It has been our purpose to put pedagogy on a foundation of practicality, as well as of scheduled observation and a lively and loving thinking approach to scientific anthropology.

There can be a parting of minds here, for those who hold that love has nothing to offer scientific thinking will scarcely gain much from this book, which is a follow-up of my previous writings. This is especially true in the case of the chapter, "A Short Expedition into the Realm of Sense-Doctrine," which appeared in my recently published study, *The Riddle of Fear*.

– Henning Köhler, M.D.
Nurtingen/Wolfschlugen
Germany

I.

FUNDAMENTALS OF A SPIRITUAL-EDUCATIONAL PRACTICE

My purpose in the following pages is to acquaint you with what may be an unfamiliar way of viewing problems of child development, one that seems to me highly significant from an educational standpoint as well.

We need guidelines as a basis for right action. That is always the case in life, and this holds true for education as well as in all our dealings with children. The decisive element in this is love, of course. We must not make the mistake, however, of thinking that heart and cognitive concerns are two different things; the opposite is true. If love for others is unrelated to a need to know and we base our association with them on that understanding, then that love lacks an essential element and remains fixed at the level of its first conceiving.

SLEEP'S CONTRIBUTION

Real understanding generates guiding ideas that lead us in a particular direction. If that direction is a valid one, it becomes the source of many inspirations. What we might call moral fantasy awakens and suggests ways of treating this or that situation. The intellectual consciousness that we have by day is responsible in large part for developing the right basic insight, for we need to be wide awake, sharply observant, self-critically with-holding subjective opinions, habitually research-minded, able to see the connection of things and to draw conclusions, and so on.

The practical, effective ideas and impulses needed for day-to-day procedures that we gain from such insights are not, however, usually born of our day working consciousness; they originate quite literally in night experience. Something more than ordinary logical thinking has to be involved to turn insights into creative impulses, and we could obviously not do so if we were not to sleep. On confronting a problem we say, "I need to sleep on it another night," because experience has taught us the value of doing so. We know that the question does not just dis-appear and that we practice working on it. We have all found that upon awakening the following morning, we find the solu-tion laying like a present under our pillow.

To begin with, we may carry this realization with us as an isolated insight that has nothing to do with daily life; it is scarcely practicable. We take it with us nightly into sleep, sum-moning it up again before our day-consciousness fades. Then we awaken the next morning with a totally clear idea and pur-pose, exclaiming, "I've got it! That is what I must do for my child, obviously! Why didn't I realize it long ago?"

Have you had this experience? I am sure you must have; everyone does, off and on. But we are not always aware enough to connect putting the question with receiving the answer. What do we do, for example, with the realization that a rebelling, fum-ing, uncooperative child is simply full of fear? Knowing this does not change the ever-recurring problems. However, if you form the habit of carrying out an imaging exercise for five min-utes every evening, calling up a picture of your raging, resistant child and intensively imagine yourself looking into him or her, seeing a trembling little bird fluttering panic-stricken in its cage— if you fall asleep over and over again, with this image, then, dear parents, it can happen that something begins changing in the daily pattern of problems. For you will find yourselves re-acting differently in many situations, perhaps not entirely con-sciously in the sense of a coolly calculated demand for a change of behavior, but relying rather on a new "fingertip" sense. Your subconsciousness acts as though it gets its directives from the image of the bird in its frightened fluttering, while at the same time, your conscious mind may still be puzzling over what you should do with the statement that your defiant child is acting out of fear.

Now you may find yourself gradually changing the tone of your voice in addressing your child. You speak more softly and melodically, so that your sentences no longer ring out like pistol shots. You can exert all possible instinctive pains not to expose your child to extreme impressions and to spare it hectic, noisy, unclear situations. It can easily happen, as stated above, that you are unconscious of making these changes. Other people may bring the change of tone to your awareness. You have subsequently drawn very useful practical consequences from our suggested image of the frightened bird that you summoned up nightly before you went to sleep.

It is the case in a lot of different situations: once a problem is solved, we marvel at the simplicity of the solution. The job is to find the clue!

I can tell you from many years as a medical-educational consultant that parents are not able, as a rule, to draw ordinary practical consequences from a consultant's findings (e.g., that a child falls into rages because it is frightened. They usually reply, "All right, we agreed that the cause is fear. What can we do with the information?")

Here, the consultant has two possible courses. He or she can offer the parents instruction in changing their own behavior patterns—in which case the suggestions may remain imprinted on their minds while the everyday situation may continue as before. Or else he can recommend an evening practice: "Daily, before sleeping, immerse yourself briefly in picturing your child as a small bird fluttering in panic in its cage. That is the inner aspect of its raging and rebelling. Then wait to see what instruction the imaging offers you."

What can be achieved in this way is naturally much richer, more and more deeply grounded, than any head knowledge one might try convulsively to translate into action, action taken mostly in vain. You experience how an insight, one that you are neither able nor willing to put into immediate practice but rather continue to "meditate" on as a questioning carried into sleep, works formatively, reshaping the structure of your habits. And you experience, too, how you are enabled to read the "answer" in your own changing conduct. It is an answer you could not have found by any amount of merely theoretical searching.

Notice that you are dealing here with a primal phenomenon that offers you a method that can be developed and built into a psychological tool.

I might be allowed to comment that seducers and rat-catchers of every stripe resort to this method of a systematic appeal to the subconscious. It depends on one's nature and purpose which sources are tapped; these can differ widely. We are concerned here with a totally selfless method, dedicated to serving mankind—in this case, children. Therefore, we call upon a wisdom that lives deep within us, a wisdom not available to waking consciousness. This must be done consciously, with clarity, avoiding any trace of egotism, seeking the help of our cognitive forces. These are requirements for putting our questions properly. Only those who know how to ask receive answers.

Does the angel answer?

Guidelines in the form of ideas are indeed a necessity! It is they that lead us to the image formed in meditative questioning and that are carried into sleep with us.

To have concerned oneself with the anthropological (or anthroposophical) background of children's developmental crises is not only advisable, but absolutely essential. But that is not enough, for it remains head knowledge, and we are at once confronted with the need to take a further step.

Where educating children is concerned, the next step consists in developing living images, lively-pictured questions suggested by scientific study, and bringing them to the beings and forces to which we are joined in the nighttime.

Finding answers by this method has to be based upon genuine interest and involvement; we must be really stirred by a desire to understand the child's being. We will, as a rule, succeed in getting what sleep has to offer only if we have done a thorough job of preparation. The subconscious is not a bargain basement for inspiration!

You can see from my example of the frightened bird that nothing in the least mystical or otherwise unusual is involved in my saying that we can get suggestions for action from our sleep— in fact, I am asserting that we are always receiving them more or less consciously. But it nevertheless touches upon a theme of great importance that deserves fuller exploration. I will gladly admit my conviction that there is something behind the suggested procedure that you may dismiss as childish, and it is that, but in a positive and serious sense. For behind it lies the possibility of getting in touch with the child's guardian angel; we encounter the angel in our sleep, if we make the necessary provisions for it in full consciousness.

The term "angel" may disturb you. We could agree on a less bothersome term, though why do we need to? A strange modern embarrassment stands in the way of opening ourselves to imaginations; instead, we allow everything to be dragged down to the level of gray, lifeless conceptualizing. Abstract scientific terminology is particularly out of place in discussing children. But please understand me: I am not using the term angel symbolically or metaphorically; I am completely serious and beg you to take it literally. In speaking of imaginations, I am not referring to fantasies, but to facts.

It was important for the evolution of consciousness that the place once held by fact-based images of invisible realities came to be occupied for the time being by logical thinking, though we had to pay for it by giving up a large chunk of livelier understanding. It is worth the trouble, now that we are equipped with objective thinking and do not need to surrender any part of it, to find our way again to those great archetypes, of which the angel is one. This can be done philosophically, taking the path of critical scientific discussion by examining whether there is any reason to assign more truth to a scientific approach than, for example, to theological, mystical, or esoteric concepts, insofar as these latter hold up just as well in active life. There is an amazing movement of sound findings on this score. But our task here cannot consist in commenting on the pros and cons of this theoretical debate. I will take the liberty of simply asserting that to assume that angels exist can be very useful under certain circumstances, and that our practically-oriented approach accords very well with such an assumption. We should put it to the test.

Let us assume, then, that it is true that we can approach a child's innermost being and real needs in sleep. As we experience that this is indeed a possibility, properly prepared for, I cannot believe that you parents and I will find ourselves, even in our most self-congratulatory subconsciousness, to be the sensationally clever creatures we would like to be. It is rather my belief that the wisdom of sleep referred to is a more complicated matter, involving as it does a "social wisdom" that teaches us to transform our loving feelings into deeds of love. I am convinced that it is the child itself that supplies us with clues in the night— not the everyday child we are familiar with, but a child on a different level of its being than the one immediately confronting us in daily life. We can call it the child's higher self, wherein what is already present as a seed will later live out the self's biography.

But a "higher self" is again nothing but a conceptual construction that drags down what is meant into an abstract generality; it could refer to almost anything. However, if we begin living and working with the idea that every individual is accompanied by a lofty being that guides his destiny and to whom he belongs with the most significant aspects of his personality, there comes a growing need to contribute to the rehabilitation of the angel image. Then one has no further desire to pander to the convention of the time by avoiding the topic. "Angels are invisible, hence accessible to thinking experience only. That experience doesn't force itself upon us, however. We have to seek it actively," writes Michaela Glöckler in her book *A Guide to Child Health*. We have to give the phenomenon its right name and deal consciously with it. There is no other way to approach the experience. Angels do not answer if our questioning looks for abstract psychodynamic implications supposedly operating automatically at an equally abstract unconscious level.

You will notice that I have made a slight correction. When I spoke before of these matters, I used the term "subconscious." That was a provisional concession to current usage. There is, of course, a subconscious, but the concept our time has of it contributes very little to understanding the phenomenon we are concerned with here.

So let us not talk today of some episode or impulse that originates in the subconscious and supplies the motivation that shapes our lives, but speak rather of the angel. That is simpler and more beautiful and exact.

A child's angel can give you practical suggestions as you sleep if you approach this being with questions framed with all possible clarity and felt by you to be extremely important. You may not discover answering directives in yourself as a thought content, but rather in the form of new impulses and motives, as an exceedingly subtle change of approach, as a growing ability to react correctly in critical situations, and so on. Practicing the art of questioning (you will remember that we discussed the possibility of putting questions in the form of images), submitting yourself in this sense to a certain amount of effort, you create what we might call receptive organs for the angel's messages. We can think of ourselves in this respect as illiterates just starting out on the job of learning our letters. But never mind—it is only by beginning that we have a hope of eventually learning to read fluently. And it is not at all hard to start. Let me again quote Michaela Glöckler: "Every plea concerned not with egotistic wishes for oneself but with a genuine desire that a child's destiny arrive at fulfillment of its own goals" is a request that the angel responds to.

QUESTIONS POSED BY THE WATCHMAN ON THE BRIDGE

Imagine yourself stepping onto a bridge as you fall asleep, and having an opportunity to relate to your child's angel at the bridge's far end. Then picture a watchman posted there whom you have to justify your crossing to. What do you suppose he would ask you?

His first question would be, "Are you bringing a clearly thought-out problem that concerns you deeply for the child's sake rather than a problem of your own?" His second question, one that may surprise you, would be, "Have you formed a really clear image of the child?"

What does a really clear image mean? Under what conditions does that clear image form itself as one falls asleep? It happens gently as the result of having taken the trouble to observe the child keenly and lovingly at least once a day and to do so, as Rudolf Steiner put it, "with reverence for the child."

One aspect of loving is the ongoing practice of overcoming one's own habitual judgments, desires, expectations, and concepts, pushing them out of the way and giving oneself instead to listening and observing in what might be called an ever-marveling attentiveness to the phenomenon of the child's image in the *here and now*, every least detail of which deserves your whole-hearted and nonjudgmental interest. At moments like these, such a reaction as, for example, annoyance that the child walks without lifting his feet properly, is completely out of place. You note instead that is his own particular way of walking. When you begin to feel a kind of tenderness awakening in you for the child's very faults and weaknesses, for all the things that ordinarily lead to strife and anger, you will know that you are on the right path.

These are the two questions asked by our imaginary bridge watcher that we parents need to prepare ourselves to be able to say "yes" to. You can do this in the following way: abstaining as far as possible from hand wringing or resentment at your lack of ability, busying yourself with unflagging efforts to understand your child's particular set of problems. Regard as less important the annoyance felt by you or reported by neighbors, or the child's teachers, concentrating instead on its self-caused miseries (for you know there is a big difference between the things we would like a child to get over because he is hurting himself and those that make us nervous or violate our principles). You can and will reach a point where you sense that you understand your child's trouble, not perhaps in every detail and final consequence, but you become aware that you have reached as far as cognition can go, the tip of the problem.

Let us take an example: You will see that on some days your child behaves as though he literally wants to jump out of his skin. Now there is a difference between regarding this as pure impudence, feeling oneself personally attacked and realizing in observant objectivity that at such times the child cannot manage his body properly and feels himself strangled and physically cooped up. You note his pale face and spotty skin and the way he moves, fighting restriction, probably complaining, too, about stupid tight clothing, though the clothes may not actually be tight.

This provides you with an image: you see that the soul experiences itself in its body just like being in frightfully uncomfortable clothing, jammed in, as though itching unbearably from contact with some material or other. Can children be expected to behave nicely and pleasantly on such occasions?

You see that when you are prompted by observations of this kind to pay more attention to nutritional matters and to seek professional advice (for it is natural to think that today's children may be eating things that could set up internal irritation in them), it is not a question of your personal preferences, dislikes or principles influencing you to reduce the intake of sweets or animal protein; you are making your decision solely on the basis of protecting the child from harming himself. You are not asking out of annoyance at having such an independent, difficult child to bring up; you are asking, with full acceptance of the degree of patience needed by the child for his personal development, whether, when he's having to behave badly when he really wants to be pleasant, this is only because his own body is his constant enemy, and he therefore needs your help. That is the first item.

IS THE BODY TOO CHILLY FOR THE SOUL?

The further requirement is that in addition to nutritional questions you make yourself a picture of "a soul squeezed into a body" as described, and regularly carry this image with you as a questioning into sleep. The watcher on the bridge will accept this as a pass if you meet the second condition, that of never failing in faithful observation of the child. It is not my intention to make a hard and fast rule of the above example, chosen at random, as a source of insights derived from meditative practice, but simply to illustrate with a small illustration of what I have in mind.

When a soul feels itself jammed too tightly into a body, the simple conclusion must be that the soul is too big to fit. So it would naturally tend to be pressed against the confining bodily boundary, unable to get through it, feeling the body to be a dam blocking it.

Now observe the child's motions when he is acting up. You will see him continually stretching and twisting, occasionally pulling himself convulsively together and then shaking himself loose again. There can be no question that you see here a blocked condition in which something inward is seeking to get free; the boundary presented by the body is too rigid and impermeable for the child's subjective feeling. It needs to be more elastic and permeable, a "breathing" border, if it is to form a suitable enclosure for the child's inner life to expand in.

What could be the reason for a child's experiencing his body as a block in every attempt to enter into relationship with the surrounding world? You already possess the image of a soul that becomes too large for the body. And you now possess the image of the impermeable bodily boundary. That is quite a lot to go on! But wouldn't it be natural for you now (at night you meditate on the above two, perhaps not technically scientific images, but nevertheless still based upon exact observation) gradually to note an instinctive need awakening in you to find out whether your child is always warm enough? You suddenly notice that the child's hands and feet are always cold. This may start at first with just an opinion that you are becoming edgy about heat, perhaps, and making the whole family nervous about it. Then you try to understand what is going on. Now you see the corrections needed.

The immediately obvious fact is that cold has some connection with rigidity and impermeability, warmth with mobility, permeability, and elasticity. Things of a soul nature burgeon in warmth, whereas the natural tendency of the physical body is to coldness. The soul can pervade the body properly only by warming it through and through. If this is not achieved from within, the warming process has to be supported from without. Warmth has a desire to expand, and the soul is similar in harboring this desire. The whole material world would stiffen and petrify if there were no such things as warmth. Our human soul-life stands in the same relationship to our physical body, being both contained within it and at the same time pressing beyond

10

the boundary it presents. If the physical body is too strongly subjected to the cold process, the soul element is not just kept within proper bounds (as it should be), but blocked in its need to expand. The child experiences this blockage as painful, particularly in developmental phases in which the soul feels a regular need to live out a dynamic, expansive relationship to the surrounding world. This is experienced in the fourth and fifth years, for example, and later on in the eighth and ninth years, before the introverted pre-pubertal phase sets in.

Now, as the parent in our example, the time has come to ask yourself a further question: What can I be doing in daily life, in a one-on-one relationship, to support my child in his or her need?

Of course, you have to go on supplying warmth from outside; that is the right thing, and helpful, but it is only treating a symptom. How does it happen that many children today prefer to feel cold? Could it be that they are comfortable when their soul is cool and contracted within their body and uncomfortable when their soul expands in warmth and wedges itself against the confining limits of their impermeable bodily boundary?

A COOL HAND AND A WARM HEART

Now, since I'm not giving a series of recipes, let's take a situation from life and say that you suddenly become uncomfortable over a fact that you previously greeted: your child is uncommonly bright; you used to comfort yourself with it when the going got hard, saying, "Well, in spite of everything, I have an unusually brilliant, talented child. At age five, she can add two-column figures in her head faster than many children years her senior." You were proud of this until now, and your pedagogical efforts tended largely in the direction of appealing to the child's mental powers, explaining and giving reasons for everything. That may have helped on some occasions, but not on others. Now you suddenly feel it is an untrustworthy procedure. You note, as you read books and newspapers, how consistently you encounter statements linking purely mental insight with a cold approach, and how well-founded the term "intellectual coldness" is. You cannot get over the feeling that the constant peripheral chilliness your child evidences may well have to do with the fact that such exceptionally bright children suffer from a stunted development of intellectual coolness.

It is certainly not my intention to say anything in the least negative about analytical thinking; it is an accomplishment, the not-least-significant aspect of which is that the soul element, the whole sphere of emotions and moods is as though repressed and held back in the thinker. That is the only way the thinker can succeed in doing it.

To think clearly and logically requires inhibiting feeling and confronting the world in a focused state. Popular talk of "a cool head" is a way of saying that rejection of the warmth activity that rises from the emotional sphere to the head, that is, to the sense organization, is essential to orderly thinking. Mental clarity demands a distancing of oneself from one's own soul life, on the one hand, and from one's surroundings, on the other. Just try to grasp a clear thought with your hand touching a hot light bulb, or to form a distinct picture of what is going on around you.

It is absolutely essential in life to master our feelings and to learn to confront the world outside in a focused, gathered state of being so that our heads can function freely. That is a necessity not to be scorned. But the process cannot be described without picturing the setting up of a cold zone between the world and oneself founded on suppressing emotional warmth. That is an inevitable accompaniment of the intellectual process. So when children are prematurely involved in the intellectual realm, you have continually to overcome the chilliness that stands in the way of contact with their surroundings. And when you also consider the fact that younger children are more open, immediately their soul-spiritual condition expresses itself in their bodily functions (and vice versa); then you will find yourself dealing with chill-related problems of restlessness and cramping that most assuredly go unrecognized in today's academic lexicon. You begin to realize that there are age levels in which the described suppressing of soul warmth is extremely damaging. It works directly counter to a child's developmental needs.

You may come to see that providing external physical warmth alone does not fill the bill. You'll need to think more about soul-warming educational approaches and attitudes, putting affectionate bodily contact ahead of verbal communication, involving the child in creative activity, singing together, playfully transforming his tendency for cramped movement into pleasure in musical-rhythmical motion. Or, instead of "sensible" instruction, make stories full of rich pictures that develop insight by means of fantasy rather than of intellect. Fantasy warms even the fingertips, whereas reason chills. If it is a child's desire to go beyond the narrow boundary of his bodily being with his impulses for fantasy and creativity, we shall not encourage elements that make that boundary only the more immobile. Your job is literally to entice the child's inner warmth forces right out to his skin, into his fingertips.

I wanted to illustrate with this example what progress you can make if you approach matters as described, with courage born of insight, and pay attention to the inspiration you receive. These are reliable guides, provided you have crossed sleep's threshold with both a clearly formed question and a distinct image of the child. Three things are essential in seeking collaboration with the child's angel: your own thoughtful effort in forming a concept of the course of human maturation; exact observation, carried on with veneration for the child; and lastly, relegating night after night, the fruits of these efforts to sleep as you prepare for it, trying yet again to combine what you have observed with insights you have arrived at.

Let us avoid any misunderstanding. It is certainly wise, occasionally, to seek a pediatrician's or educational consultant's advice when some aspect of your child's behavior makes you feel unsure of yourself. On the other hand, every achievement of independence from the "experts" who are available nowadays for help in every conceivable kind of problem means a significant gain in freedom, self-confidence, and a calmness that is transmitted to the child as well. And I am convinced that "experts" in educational matters should undertake each job with a conscious intention to make themselves superfluous.

Please take what I have been saying as offered in just that sense.

WHAT CONSTITUTES MORAL EDUCATION?

Allow me, in what follows, to deal with some phenomena of child development that seem to me to be receiving much too superficial attention from current academic psychology and educational science. I propose, in so doing, that we agree to continue accepting the hypothesis of children's guardian angels on a working basis, in order to become at home with a way of thinking which assumes their involvement to be a fundamental fact.

Let us explore the characteristics of a guardian angel as it watches over a child and is active within it.

It is a being that has taken on the task of helping a child, in the course of his or her personality development, to grow ever stronger in forming ideals and becoming idealistically motivated, providing the impulses needed to overcome the conflict between individual striving and social responsibility. It is the angel's activity in a child's growing-up that leads the child to begin concerning himself with a humane and charitable approach to his fellows and to feel the first stirring of caring and a selfless readiness to help; this cannot be ascribed solely to the effects of our authoritarian moralizing, as psychoanalysts would have us believe. Both backgrounds play a part, of course; children do learn the social virtues from observing the behavior of the adults they copy. But how do they come to feel for those virtues? Just to hear themselves praised? Those who think so are habitual materialists in their thinking rather than realists taught by experience.

Rudolf Steiner had good cause to assert consistently and firmly that preaching and insisting on morality was not only useless, but actually harmful when considered as a means of developing a dependable morality for later life. Morality fostered through preaching breeds opportunism; it hinders the development of an autonomous morality that rises to the height of creating autonomous ideals.

An educational method based on teaching children that more can be gained then lost by sacrifice puts the capacity for altruism, inborn in human nature and pressing for expression, in a depressingly false light. If, for example, we let a child sense that she can profit from magnanimous giving or an uncomplaining nature, that certain benefits accrue from putting others' needs and demands before her own, we supply her with anything but good motivation. The virtue of consideration for others is dragged down to the level of a school report and correspondingly rewarded or punished. This handling can be equated with pressure for moral accomplishment. Rather than furthering social sensitivity, it encourages a species of slyly calculated diplomacy totally devoid of social caring.

We see, therefore, that an education that moralizes is a contradiction in terms. The development of interpersonal social values and attitudes in childhood is, by definition, a mere conforming to adult expectation and overlooks an absolutely decisive fact: there is nothing of a moral nature in mere conformity on the social level; it can at best be termed pseudo morality.

Of course, one might raise the objection, "well then so be it"; there is only pseudo morality.

There is no use letting oneself in for endless discussion; it is a waste of time. Let us stick instead with observations of living reality and ask what moves a child that is not subjected to "moral education" by precept to develop imitative feeling for social values that are real rather than demanded.

Living examples are decisive here! But even that would be ineffective if children did not possess an inherent capacity to appreciate the conduct witnessed and, with joy, make it their own way of behaving, totally uninfluenced by any expectation of benefits that would be forthcoming to them. This is an example of having an inner affinity for what is good in the world, and it is not a taught lesson. It depends on education whether this basic and, as-yet-undefined tendency to love the good, finds proper outlets, even though education is not its source. Education can only spell its ruin.

Just notice the shining eyes of children listening to a telling of the legend of Good Roland, or of St. Nicholas, or to stories in which "the good person" rises to heroic stature. Observe the pride and delight with which elementary school pupils react to accounts of "good deeds" done by their parents. Parental misdeeds call forth no such reactions. And do not make the mistake of thinking that the inner rejoicing experienced by children listening to tales of admirable human beings that cause their eyes to lighten up can be accounted for by any moral teaching they have received. We understand less than nothing if we persist in explaining soul phenomena as the outcome of such simplistic motivation.

Perceiving as a cosmic-creative process

We can see angels at work in children's imitative inclination to the good. But angels have to join forces with a child's parents in preparing the right conditions for this activity. It will at once be apparent that the preparation they make has nothing in common with what is usually thought of as moral or ethical teaching.

I must say again that an absolutely basic educational principle is involved here: namely, that moral education, rightly understood, must not be of an instructional nature, at least not in the first twelve years of a child's life. It must rather consist of creating the preconditions that enable a child to transform his inborn affinity to the good. This began as the child's needs and demands on the surrounding world evolved and developed into a capacity for social perceptiveness and moral impulse. Much is involved here that usually goes unnoticed.

The aesthetics active in human community are not a mysterious, loosely-swirling element, but one requiring perceptive and expressive organs. I will take an example from another realm of life to explain what I mean. Consider the fact that you are able to appreciate the world's beauty only because you possess sense organs constructed to convey it. In the case of seeing and hearing, we take this for granted. Human beings first approach the sphere of beauty as perceivers and enjoyers and then, in their capacity to imitate, which can develop later into free creativity, become producers themselves in that sphere. We can see in this case how cultivation of our senses provides the basis for an inflowing of right impulses, which translate into active expression. That is because the perceptive activity in which the soul engages is by its very nature creative. When the sight of a rosebush arouses a sense of delight in us, we call it "beautiful." We feel personally affected, indeed almost proud, not because we derive our delight from the external rosebush, but because we recreate it in ourselves in perceiving it. We are overjoyed that we are able to bring a rosebush into being! We have eyes to see, which obviously has something to do with the soul's deeply implanted need to create, to be creatively active. The sharp demarcation we draw between perceiving and carrying out some activity is based on theory rather than on reality, for in our tissue the boundaries are fluid. Our sense organs serve us like "receptacles" or vessels in which the in-flowing outer world is subjected to a kind of higher chemical process; impressions are "killed off," destroyed, and then built up anew.

That is the process that every conscious act of perceiving undergoes in our contact with the world around us. Human beings are not camera-like reflectors. We have to reproduce on our own everything we want to become aware of; otherwise, everything would be wiped out in forgetfulness.

It is upon this productive activity, in which we derive experiences from perceptions, that we base all the creative artistry that we develop as skills in life. We discover in early childhood's urge to initiate the roots of the art of destroying and recreating that lifts *perceiving* to the level of a world-creating process. It shouldn't be mistaken for an automatic copying or mere reflecting of the external scene. Quite the contrary! Images and sounds, and so on, transmitted by a particular scene undergo a complete transformation. What issues from it—despite any deceptive similarity—is something entirely different from the original sense impression. It can be compared in a way to the impressive naturalistic painting once so popular. If, for example, the tree painted with such faithful detail on the linen had been a mere imitation of the actual tree, we would have to ask what the point of painting it is, since the original is so far superior to the copy. But that was not at all what painters of a serious naturalistic school were trying to accomplish. They were revealing to us the secret of the creative act attendant to the process of perceiving, the secret of an inner happening, known to all of us, and rendered visible in being lifted to the conscious level. That was necessary as a prelude to advancing to a truly free aesthetic art wherein the artist claims the freedom not to recreate the perceived image on the basis of an external model, but rather to play with single elements of destroyed images and compose them into a new grouping not to be found in the objective world. Or, these elements may be used simply to document the destructive process itself.

IMITATION AND YEARNING FOR THE GOOD

The relationship of imitation to the arts is not our theme, however. So let us leave it at the point we have reached, and hold on to the finding that "the feeling for beauty has nothing to do with value judgments or aesthetic categories, but rather with the fact that we human beings experience ourselves as creating reality in our sense-activity." Creativity awakens in our imitative inclination to experience what the world presents to us, not with the small child's concern with his own self, as popular psychoanalysis still obstinately asserts.

But psychoanalysts, too, have got hold of a corner of the truth in their apprehension of the fact that art must have something to do with destination and transformation of the external scene. Something comparable occurs in the metabolizing of foods. Farfetched analogies of this sort are the result of proceeding on the hypothesis that soul-spiritual phenomena are to be understood, in principle, as modifications of phenomena that are bodily in origin.

We do not accept this view as a working hypothesis, the worst shortcoming of which is that it is impractical. Our stand is taken on the ground that the largest proportion of the foods we consume are unusable by the body, and, therefore, has to be excreted; bowel movements have neither lesser nor greater significance. They have as little do with creativity as coughing has to do with recitation of poetry.

But the imitating of early childhood, which offers a truly far greater experience of pleasure than all performances put together, has very much to do with creativity. It relates impressions and expressions. Not only is it the first manifestation of the shaping will, but it is also the most decisive step in sense-maturation, in the ability to make a proper use of sense-impressions. Rudolf Steiner, in his book *The Social Question*, says that

18

the seed of freedom lies in imitation. That may sound paradoxical. But what we have just been discussing may be some help in grasping its truth. I can assure you from many years' experience as a remedial worker and medical-educational consultant that there is a striking connection between restlessness and poor concentration in children who, for whatever reason, have done too little imitating in their first four or five years. Therapy, in the case of these jumpy, nervous children, consists of exposing them to an intensive makeup course in imitation that includes pantomime, recitation, rhythmic activities, copying all sorts of sounds, and the like. Much can be accomplished at home, too, with such activities; as I have said, "experts" are not the only resource. Set aside one-half hour three times a week to work with your wiggleworm, and play games that stimulate him to imitate. That way, you gradually smooth his path to the deeper creative playing needed in developing concentration and in carrying out his school responsibilities. You will make much more progress doing these things than subjecting him to tutoring or constant moralizing. And turn off the TV. It is one of the worst enemies of wholesome imitation.

But let us turn now from the subject of aesthetic feeling and the will to create beauty that has served us merely as an example, and return to what we called children's imitative readiness to favor the good. It is true on this level, too, though not quite as obvious, that perceptive organs have to be developed. Later on, the impressions derived from an inclination or affinity to the good gives rise to independent creative will impulses, provided that that affinity—or, to put it another way, the child's trust or confidence—is not misused as a means of moral training. It has been explained that in witnessing goodness, experienced as love in the deeds and words and behavior patterns of others, something in a child responds with deep satisfaction, and that this response, still quite undefined as to content, is a little "educated" as, for example, pleasure in a flowering meadow or gaily colored ball. Children would have to be taught not to enjoy colorful toys if that were deemed desirable, so great is the natural pleasure they take in them, whether we approve or not.

But we rob them of that pleasure if we give them too much of it. That forces them to deaden themselves to the pull of sensationally over-colorful, glittering, loud playthings we mistakenly overload them with. Boredom and indifference are the outcome, and the budding artist in a child is on the road to ruination.

Children's capacity for love is also undermined if we respond to the wondering openness of the good that they bring into life with constant instruction, moral appeals, and pious phrases. These too breed indifference; they are all useless. What does matter is setting an unobtrusive example in our own way of living.

Certain perceptive capacities are essential to a proper grasp of this exemplary relating, so that it may be tied with inner participation and made our soul possession, freely disposed of. Furthermore, those perceptive capacities are identifiable. We can begin by describing how children's angels work with parents and others involved to awaken such capacities. I am counting on your openness to attempt to describe them.

There is an aspect of anthroposophical anthropology related particularly to child development which, thus far, all too little attention has been paid. That is an extended study of the basis of a science of the senses by Rudolf Steiner. Let us keep in mind that angels have been described here as beings whose longing is to enable mankind to form ideals and to become capable of moral fantasy. They want to pour impulses of love into human souls.

Let us now ask what the nature of their activity is as they strive to achieve this in the "receptacle forming" of early childhood.

2.

Exploring the Life Sense

Introduction

In the course of Rudolf Steiner's researches on the human sense organization, he discovered twelve aspects which he characterized as senses. He defined "sense" as any perceptive capacity whereby we gain direct information as to what is going on in and around us without relying on our thinking about it. When, for example, we look at a tree and establish the fact that it is a tree, this determination and any feelings it calls forth in us are related to the sense impression, but the concept is not the sense-impression as such. There is a decisive difference—one we need to keep clearly in mind. Otherwise, we would have to say that a child is too young to be able to form concepts or judgments and receives no sense impressions. That would obviously be nonsense.

We cannot completely cover the area of all twelve of the senses here and can touch only on the most salient aspects of those we will be exploring.[1] For clarity's sake, three "sense-areas" need to be distinguished, as Rudolf Steiner showed. The first group is the so-called physical or basal senses (also called "will-related senses"). Next come the psychic or feeling-related senses of smell, taste, vision, and warmth. Thirdly, the "social" or "higher" senses that relate us to our fellow humans, which, though definitely not responsible for thinking as such, have a close connection to our thinking and conceptual life. These are the senses of hearing, speech, thought, and the ego sense. Readers interested in pursuing these matters will find them covered in the collected works of Rudolf Steiner.

Now some of you may be surprised that in discussing the development of children's social capabilities, I omit any commentary on the so-called social senses in favor of concentrating on the basal senses (which might also be termed "self-perceptive senses"). But do not forget that our present concern is with the angel's "receptacle-creating" activity, which is the preliminary to later achievement of genuine social participation and possible selflessness in a person's awareness of her fellow-beings, sensitizing her to others' way of speaking and thinking and to her perception of their unique individuality. That calls for a good deal of labor-filled preparation.

BASIC WELL-BEING

I will depart from the usual habit of beginning an enumeration of the senses with the sense of touch and start instead with the vital or life sense. In my view, thorough observation of child development justifies terming this the fundamental sense, although it is the hardest to describe from a developmental-psychological angle.

Now what are we to understand by the term "life sense"?

Rudolf Steiner answers: "Our first perception of our human selves is conveyed by the life sense, which makes us conscious of ourselves as complete incorporate entities."

The emphasis here is on an experience of completeness, our very first one of this kind, and one that is transmitted to our consciousness by our bodies. A child "listening" to his own body gradually gets a feeling of intimacy with it that conveys a first still-dreaming sense of identity. Children feel secure and sheltered inside their bodies. Rudolf Steiner once described this as a state of "feeling comforted and comfortable through and through," of a being at home in oneself that is a fundamental orientation in life; all other later orientations build on this. So there is clearly a significant lack of orientating capacity in children whose sense of shelter and well-being has been damaged, and their early years are naturally continuously vulnerable on this score. Every species of bodily disturbance has a disorienting effect on the life sense, concretely expressed, a distorted perception. This is especially true during the period in which the basal or fundamental senses have not reached full development and are, therefore, in a correspondingly labile state.

This holds true for later life as well, except that adults are usually able to maintain their concept of reality to some extent even when the life sense is disturbed in its momentary functioning by pain or illness. This is chiefly due to the fact that, with the passage of time, the life sense is extended, taking on a temporal sensitivity in addition to its earlier general corporeal experiencing; a sensing of oneself as the continuity of one's own life path develops. We are, therefore, justified in referring to the life sense as the "biographical sense," and it can go on functioning as such even when bodily perception is impaired.

That does not apply, however, in the case of very young children. In their case, the life sense has to be conceived as purely corporeal, keeping in mind that this sense needs all the more careful nurturing to make sure it fulfills its eventual biographical functioning.

What must be done to ensure this?

Allow me to add some clarifying comments on the primary functioning of the life sense. To take hearing as an example, we know that shrill and excessively loud noises and a confusion of sounds irritate the sense rather than appeal to it, as a pleasing phrase of music does. The life sense is similarly affected; feelings of discomfort grate on the body, disturbing it. But it is "in its element" when, as it listens to its body, it finds it in a fundamentally peaceful, harmonious condition.

Every sense function has a dynamic goal, in that all perceptive activity is linked with unconscious expectation of finding what we are looking for in the perceptive field. This dynamic, this launching-toward-a-goal, always fits the orientating function of a particular sense. We normally become aware of it only when our goal is not achieved. The orientating help that we expect from our eyes as a matter of course comes to consciousness only if we suddenly experience difficulty in seeing, in double vision, for example, or as the result of a shifting perspective. Such disturbances do occur, and they can be considerably unsettling. Just as we have to have opened our eyes to be aware of a difficulty in seeing, so the life sense that is constantly listening to the condition of our bodies has to convey information of organic indispositions. But we become aware of these not as expected perceptions of the part of the life sense, but as irritations within the perceptive fields themselves. Our human senses serve not only as means of registering facts, but above all in assuring us (after the fact) of the durability and reliability of our existence.

This is particularly evident in the case of the life sense. Its primary activity is providing continuous information as to whether our body fundamentally offers the supporting security and harmony necessary to smooth personality development in undisturbed intercourse with the surrounding world.

The secondary function of the life sense is to supply awareness of any threatening or disquieting ups and downs of the body. When these occur, there is a momentary switching on of waking consciousness, and it seeks ways of restoring the pure sense function (the expected state). If there is internal pain or bodily distress, then quoting Rudolf Steiner, "the life sense, ordinarily experienced as a feeling of well-being, is disturbed in the way an external sense is when, for example, a hearing problem exists." The life sense does the orientating task assigned to it only (to quote Rudolf Steiner again), "when its activity, rayed into the soul, is felt to be permeated by well-being."

This definition must be kept in mind to avoid the mistaken concept that the task of the life sense is to perceive the processes that disturb it. Hans Schenrle hit upon just the fitting description with his term, "sense of well-being."

FURTHER THOUGHTS ON THE DIFFICULT THEME, LIFE SENSE

The objection was made in a recent discussion that it would be just as justified to speak of a "sense of non-well-being" as it is to speak of a "sense of well-being." But that is only partly true. If we ask what the nature of a perceptive field should be for the sense directed upon it to assure us of ideal orientation in our perceiving of it, we realize that the most favorable state for, say, the sense of sight to operate in is that of tempered moderate brightness. The most favorable state for the life sense's functioning is similarly a well-tempered, calm sensing of the body. The sense of sight is diminished by relative darkness, suspended in the total absence of light, and irritated by exposure to blinding light. That is equally true in the case of the life sense. When there is a lowered or extensively obscured body sensing (as, for example, in a drugged condition), that sense too is diminished, suspended, or made uncomfortable (always signifying "excessively aware") and irritated in its body consciousness. We feel ourselves properly orientated in the perceptive field of the life sense when our sensing of the body is unobtrusively well-tempered and peaceful. In my book, *The Riddle of Fear*, I pointed out that this sensation is sleep related, that the life sense's perceiving is akin to those aspects of our nature that are to some extent still asleep when we are awake. We must not let ourselves confuse the term "life sense" with the popular concept of "vitality" as a state of wide-awakeness, liveliness, freshness. It is true that the life sense is responsible in large part for feelings of energy and freshness, but that is due to a subconscious sensing that there is peace and warmth and well-being deep down inside our bodies. That accounts for our sense of a vital condition. Like flowers that have to be rooted in warm, well-watered, well-aerated soil in order to open to the sun, what we sense as vitality is rooted in that well-tempered, quiet bodily awareness, and offers itself to the ego's use. As a rule, energy and freshness well up in the morning, after restorative sleep out of the sphere of the life sense, though that is not their only source. In the evening, when we tend to feel more settled, that sense of burgeoning vitality disappears, but without any ill effect on the basic sensation of security mediated by the life sense. Except in conditions of poor health, that security is threatened only when, instead of giving in to the need to rest (which is actually a need to devote ourselves to the sphere of the life sense by ceasing all energy-demanding activity, both physical and mental), we force ourselves to stay awake. The other bodily senses (those of taste, motion, and balance) are obviously already dimmed in ordinary states of weariness, but the life sense is not. It is quite in its element when we give in to sleepiness and a "settled" feeling; at such times disintegrative processes are reduced to a minimum, giving regenerative processes the upper hand. Only in cases of utter exhaustion resulting from real abuse of the vital forces does a disturbance of the life sense, signaled by an inability to sleep despite deep weariness, surface. When an easy falling asleep takes place, the life sense assumes responsibility for the entire sense organism. It is that sense the basic functioning of which remains unaffected by the alternation of sleeping and waking. Feelings of energy and freshness are messages beamed into the soul's awareness by the life sense as it reports on the amount of energy stored in its subterranean reservoir, in the realm where we are still asleep after waking up, despite increased organic wear and tear due to the bodily and mental activities of waking life. Up-building and enlivening processes are fed from the "region of sleep."

Those up-building processes will be referred to here as "ordering harmonizing" in contrast to constituting the perceptive field of the life sense. Life forces that shoot into a random, disorderly burgeoning are not included in the definition; they irritate the life sense.

The sensing of vigor and freshness is due to further influences, as we shall see—influences coming from the night-side of experience and responsible firstly for building up sensations of touch, giving form and configuration; secondly, for providing control in motion (freeing and coordinating); thirdly, ensuring body-soul balance, upright stance, and walking ("lightening-integrating"). What we are concerned with here is an overall sensing of vitality, such as adequate sleep, which good health provides. It is the composite product of perceptions emanating from all the four bodily senses: well-being, stemming from the life sense; form and frame, as perceived by touch; dynamics, transmitted by the sense of motion; and the feeling of being permeated by the erective force of light with which the sense of balance endows us. Our sensing of a calm, warm, streaming life, referred to above as "basic well-being", is to be ascribed to

26

the life or vital sense. It is the fundamental source of a general sensing of vim and vigor. All body-related feelings that produce the sensation of well-being bear its signature.

THE POSITIVE, CALM WAKING STATE AND
THE COSMIC PRINCIPLE OF GOODNESS

"No one can understand the senses who isn't aware that it is possible to have an inner feeling of oneself as a completeness," Rudolf Steiner tells us. We owe our first fundamental experiencing of wholeness and continuity to the life sense, which gives growing children the agreeable sensation of inner restfulness and the security of self-containment.

This sense of being sheltered and stable, which starts with bodily self-perception, is of the utmost conceivable importance for later life. Not only does the degree of our self-confidence and trust in existence depend upon it, but also, as we have seen, it relates to our looking forward to an ongoing course of development or else facing a life that is a conglomeration of fragmented, disconnected single events.

But this sense is far from mature at birth. Quite the opposite, just observe a child in its first few months. What impresses you if you face facts squarely? Babies are so at war with their bodies that all they want to do is sleep so that they need not notice that they have bodies! There is scarcely a trace of well-being to be seen. Their bodies cause them constant annoyance.

When they are awake, very young children are either hungry or suffer from intestinal discomfort, or they are cold or sweating or miserable from dirty diapers, or the like. In any case, they are anything but happy in their bodies while awake, and peace is restored only when their parents have taken all possible measures to eliminate their bodily unease. Thereupon the child tires out. Only when asleep or on the verge of sleep does memory experience the sense of well-being that provides the life sense with orientation.

Fortunately, the situation soon changes. A few weeks later, if everything goes well, the condition called *positive peaceful waking* in developmental psychology sets in. It happens frequently that instead of starting to jerk and cry the moment she awakes, the child babbles to herself, plays with her fingers, is seemingly content with herself and the world. This teaches us that, on the one hand, the organism (which, to avoid total miscomprehension, we must accustom ourselves to grasp as an assembled rather than, superficially, as a merely biological organism) is gradually adjusting to living on earth, and, on the other hand, has developed a corresponding positive sensing of her body. This positive feeling now harbors a certain constancy and reliability, which indicate that the child can no longer be upset by such trifles as ordinary hunger or a twitching here and a tickling there. This can be taken as significant, further evidence that the life sense is now well on the way to maturity. The capacity with which this sense endows us "to have an inward sensing of ourselves as whole" (as Rudolf Steiner puts it), this fundamental body-based orientation stands up to a relatively high degree of challenge without breaking down. But the level of tolerance in cases where the life sense has been injured is much lower, requiring very little to bring about a loss of orientation. Typical cases of such injuries are on our agenda for later discussion.

At this point, babies have learned that their bodily confines, which, to begin with, they so disliked having to live, can be a cozy dwelling, even a place of pleasurable well-being.

How did they learn this? What has happened to bring about this adjusting to the earth conditions encountered by ensouled organisms at first manifestly overtaxed by these conditions?

The first answer is obvious: it was all the care and solicitous handling a baby received, all the concern for its bodily well-being. We should avoid making the mistake here of thinking that a dutiful carrying out of hygienic and medical rules and regulations could suffice in nurturing the development of the life sense. If that were possible, child therapists would have fewer problems, for every such prescribed measure could be faithfully carried out and the child so cared for could still suffer from neglect. Duty is not the issue here. The real need is for a relaxed reverential devotion to nourishing and warming acts of bodily care; they must be done with true inner participation. Caring for the life sense is not at all the same thing as bodycare. Though the sphere of a small child's experiencing is predominately that of her own body, though she lives in a state of body-mediated perception of the world around her, the experiencer and perceiver is nevertheless a soul being and as such reacts first to the *how* rather than the *what*. We educate the life sense by letting children experience goodness as a bodily condition.

The fact that a child's own body is made the home of her soul-experiencing of the universal concept "goodness," that her body is the first conveyer of human warmth, tenderness, and the like, the foundation is laid for the right basic development of the life sense. The "imitative inclination to the good" discussed above also finds therein its first ability, so laden with consequences, to orientate itself. Rudolf Steiner once described how every child harbors a profound unconscious conviction at the start of life that the world is moral through and through. It is immensely important whether this "basic assumption," as he calls it, is (or is not) confirmed in a child's first few months by her bodily sense experience.

Life rhythms and a confident stance in life

It is a fact of educational practice that a child's life sense maturing is given the right support by devoting enough attention to his bodily care, to gentle handling, to the way we feed and warm and dress him (for it makes a difference, in one's feeling for the quality of life, what one wears in contact with one's skin the whole day long). For this we need an unhurried sense, patience, foresight, a capacity for inner quiet which allows for what might be called a reverential atmosphere. We cannot always achieve it, of course, but occasional success is important. Making everyday functions rhythmical is a great help if it is done consciously rather than as an empty practice.

We might, for example, assign half an hour every evening to making an inner effort to shut out ordinary business and be there wholly present for the child, carrying out every action with true inner participation rather than as a routine matter, filling every word spoken to the child with forethought or else keeping silent, ignoring a ringing telephone, avoiding scattered thoughts, intent on registering, if only for half an hour, how wonderful it is to hold a little human being in our arms. If we undertake this every day at the same time in a rhythm consciously adopted by us, we will soon notice how beneficial it is, not only for the child but for ourselves. A mother-child relationship is established by efforts of this kind which, though relieved of everyday commonplaceness, are nevertheless perfectly consonant with everyday scheduling requirements; they actually provide the character of soul experiences and a lasting, deepening effect.

The same holds true of the father-child relationship. Fathers and mothers are both necessary, otherwise things are out of kilter. Mothers of two or three or more children should not have to listen to others' sermons about finding enough leisure and reverence if they are left to care for the whole household and the children's upbringing all by themselves.

And while we are on the subject of rhythm, everything done to bring rhythm consciously into life with children, as in the above example, has the advantage of more than just the resultant peacefulness and collectedness for the doer—it establishes a pedagogical atmosphere that has a direct effect on the rhythms inherent in children's internal organs, as well as in the sleeping-waking rhythm with its healthful action on the metabolic processes. These interrelationships should be kept firmly in mind. Roswilha Heimann's brilliant book, *Rhythm and Its Curative-Pedagogical Significance* quotes Urusla Mueller as saying, "rhythm as inner control ensures that moods and feelings, ordinarily subject to fluctuation, are forged into a lasting, fulfilling, inner possession."

In the case of very young children, the regulating of moods and feelings cannot be separated from the regulation of metabolic processes—rhythm is the chief regulating factor here. In the rhythmical organizing of life, with and around a child, you provide her body-soul individuality which is desiring of awakening to awareness of her "lastingly fulfilling inner content," which is to say her ego-consciousness, with "rhythmical training."

To be carried by life rhythms means in the fullest sense to learn to breathe. This leads not only "to an overall strengthening of the constitution," so well described in Dieter Schulz's small volume, *Frühförderung in der Heilpädagogik*, but also assists in the birthing of personality-awareness, or, more exactly, of a consciousness of personal continuity. Rudolf Steiner once expressed this as "becoming a soul in the breathing process." The rhythm of heart and breathing that gradually becomes stabilized in the course of childhood as a relatively independent personal rhythm builds the foundation for a sense of security and self-confidence. It is as essential as the physical body to sensing oneself as inwardly complete.

Neither today's children nor we adults are granted much real sharing in nature's rhythms, so the rhythmic principle has to be made a deliberate part of the pedagogical setup. This has a beneficent effect on the maturing of the life sense.

THE NERVOUS, OVERACTIVE, RESTLESS CHILD

Let us remind ourselves that unhurried peacefulness and reverential feeling are the best inner approach and support for everything we do externally in the feeding, warming, bodily care, sleep, and rhythm concerns involved in the maturing of the life sense. If these are lacking, no external setup we devise is of much use, to put it bluntly. You do not need me to tell you what rarities reverence and an unhurried dealing with things are in our time; you know it already, as I, the father of two daughters, also know from my own experience. So it isn't surprising that behavioral problems caused by lack in the development of the life sense surface as some of the weightiest faced today by parents, teachers, pediatricians, and therapists. What sort of problems are these?

It is the life sense, as we have seen, that provides the basis for the existential sense of calmness, shelter, and stability. It allows a child to experience himself as a soul within a body and as a body being energized by a soul. It mediates a basic experiencing of body-soul completeness. Permeated by well-being is, according to Rudolf Steiner, the condition toward which a child directs his expectation, his "dynamic goal", and it is the sure means of orientation in heightening the tolerance level when confronted with upsetting change. Put more simply and picturesquely, a thoroughly healthy life sense makes clear distinctions between major and minor irritations. When it is calling attention to "bodily distress," the primary perception of oneself as an experienced completeness is by no means suspended. Except in cases where bodily indispositions are overwhelming, we can, therefore, still feel ourselves standing on more or less solid inner ground. The primary perceiving afforded by the life sense demonstrates a relatively higher degree of durability than does the perceiving conveyed by the secondary life sense (in the perception of mere moods).

This does not hold true in the case of children whose life sense has suffered injury. With them, every mood instantly breaks up the inner ground of their existence. As they listen to their bodies, feelings of tension, soreness, and discomfort set in. Seldom indeed do they have the experience of "uttermost well-being" of which Rudolf Steiner speaks, and, as a rule, only at times when they are so worn out that they can no longer escape exhaustion. In the daytime, escaping exhaustion, avoiding every aspect of quietness is actually their chief occupation, for quietness focuses awareness on their own bodies; perception of the body by the life sense is enhanced. And if the sensations thus aroused are unpleasant, such children begin fidgeting, racing around, talking endlessly, prying at something, biting their nails, making faces, *ad infinitum*. They like to be in noisy, hectic surroundings, because that distracts them, and if quiet threatens to set in, they begin at once to make things noisy and hectic by their own efforts.

Children of this kind often develop nervous ticks such as conspicuous coughing or throat clearing, exaggerated blinking, jerky noddings, holding their breath, and the like. All this comes from their need to be doing something all the time so as not to have to notice their own condition. They are naturally pushovers for every kind of seductive electronic game. They seize every allowed and forbidden opportunity to eat sweets in order to get a body sensation of soul harmony, if only momentarily, not to be had without manipulation. Their parents are often disquieted by the fact that such children masturbate at every opportunity while still very young, though it should be noted that, contrary to widespread rumors, this practice in childhood is not related to sexual fantasies. These children are awkward and untidy, always bumping and hurting themselves, often seized by aggressive motor impulses. It is astonishing how little aware they are in their hectic and distraught conducting of their own bodies. A little ruffian can come home with bleeding knees without being aware of the injury; another runs around in sandals in the snow, blue-footed with cold, with no sense of distress. This neglect of the body and of its care and appearance is typical. We can almost speak of a practiced capacity to ignore the body, to "switch off" bodily sensations.

We should see this behavior-shaping (compensatory) capacity as a reaction to injury done to the orientation of the life sense. And while the sensing of the body in states of hyperactive motor unrest is greatly lessened, sensations of the organs in a quiet working state are, quite the opposite, enhanced to an extreme degree. That is why that condition is so insistently avoided. The so-called "hyperactive child" is driven by body-fear, or, more exactly, by fear of becoming attentive to his own body. The causes are to be sought in the child's first months and years of life in which the above-described developmental step that establishes a positive, peaceful working state has not been properly taken. During such a child's later years, as he grew up and developed intellectually—often to the point of outstripping his peers in this respect—he has remained, where his basic sensing of vitality is concerned, in the babyish condition of constant suffering induced by his bodily sensations. His reactions are equally delayed babyish ones: fidgeting, a constant making of noises, the ever-present need for oral gratification (only now sneaking takes the place of mother's milk). In most of the cases known to me there is also a need, bordering on a seizure-like aggressiveness, to talk foolishly. This causes a mother to withdraw in rejection with her nerves on edge.

We see how, on the one hand, these children go to all kinds of lengths to avoid having to be self-aware, because self-awareness has brought them unpleasant experiences, while, on the other hand, behaving in a manner aimed momentarily at achieving a state of harmony provides a sense of well-being in their bodies that lays the foundation for an energetic, firm soul- and will-life.

Although the portrait is not yet complete, we know the type of disturbed child whose behavior we have been discussing, children with the so-called hyperactive syndrome which orthodox science is again—thank goodness!—on the point of ceasing to call "minimal cerebral disfunction." We are speaking of nervous, unconcentrated, restless children, often of above-average intelligence and poor motor integration, children all too familiar as consistent disturbers of the peace, characters who throw sand in the works on every occasion, especially on solemn, reverential ones. They are intolerably foolish talkers, notorious babblers, but also well liked for their lightening-swift minds, original quips, and the unexpectedly stormy declarations of love they can heap on adults who have won their trust.

To sum up briefly: due to inadequate orientation in the area of their primary life sense perception, the slightest disturbing bodily sensation calls forth in these children such insecurity that they respond with behavioral anomalies of a nervous-aggressive nature caused by bodily fear. Today, more and more children lean in this direction for reasons that cannot be further discussed here.

It is not always the parents' fault that this is happening. Due to many factors, the whole background of civilization today is a troubled one. But this makes it only more necessary to address the problem and seriously seek fitting pedagogical solutions. If you take to heart the suggestions made here, you will be working for your children's future. Giving them, with real inner devotion, the care needed by the developing life sense in the way they are fed and warmed, the way their bodies are handled in all contact with them, in establishing rhythm and in seeing that they get proper sleep, you will be helping them get not only the right confidence in themselves and in life, you will be doing still more—which brings us back to where we started!

The "still more" is a way of saying that care of the life sense looks ahead to and includes the education of the moral sense as well.

FOSTERING THE LIFE SENSE AS A FREEING OF THE BREATH

We have been concerning ourselves with the fact that a child's angel is a spiritually active companion to the child on his destined path, intent upon pouring into his soul impulses of love (more popularly expressed, social capabilities) and, thus, in the child's younger years and with the help of the adults concerned, creating optimum prospects for his future.

Now what are the social capabilities for which the life sense lays the foundation?

Let me remind you, before answering this question, that children—and we adults, too—enter the angel's sphere in sleep and bring back from it certain impulses that cannot be explained in biological or socio cultural grounds—impulses that would not otherwise put in an appearance.

Allow me to tell an interesting anecdote here. Shortly before his death, the blind existentialist, Jean-Paul Sartre, gave an interview. He made an assessment of his life work and said, among other things, that as a philosopher he had "run aground on the metaphysical level," because he had "failed to find out what the source of morality was."

According to his atheistic conception of man, such a thing as God could actually not exist. Sartre had an honest, straightforward mentality. Our century would have been much poorer without him. I cannot make out why he is so little acknowledged and often even looked down upon in our circles. In that same interview he charged his followers to deal with the riddle of morality. We will be doing that to some extent here today by asking the question in a more precisely developmental-psychological form, namely: Whence comes a small child's affinity, its imitative tendency towards what's moral?

Let us risk giving an answer which, while it may not be quite to the modern taste, is one absolutely demanded by the needs of our time. It is the angel's supersensible presence expressed in the child. It is a child's remembered legacy brought with her from the prenatal life where she was in union with her angel. This affinity, this mood of expectation focused on the good, is renewed every night in the child's reunion with her angel.

How is this renewal brought about?

Angels, unlike incarnated human beings, have no knowledge of what is good, nor do they make decisions for the good. Good simply *is*. Entering the angelic sphere thus puts human souls in a situation in which they "breathe goodness" exactly as, on earth, they breathe air. On their return to earthly consciousness and conditions, they experience a feeling of missing something, a feeling of constriction, oppression, or tightness. Breathing in higher worlds is immeasurably freer and easier than here on earth. When we are asleep, body and soul both breathe at the same time. In waking life, soul and body breathe separately, with the result that we have an impression that part of us is not adequately cared for in our daytime breathing.

Such matters can, of course, be suggested only in images. But if you observe yourself keenly, you will surely agree with me when I say that we continuously suffer, when awake, from a patent deep-down feeling of "suffocation"; we accustom ourselves to it, but it is there. And this sensed deprivation, this constriction, gives rise to something we are all familiar with and of which we all say that we do not know what causes it and what it is directed toward. I refer to the sensation of longing.

Longing is, at bottom, always a longing for the good, for love and shelter. That is why it is also true that this deeply founded sense of suffocation is eased not only in sleep, but when we give or receive love and shelter in relationships with our fellow human beings.

An aspect of primal longing comes to the fore, and it is present, too, in far more obvious measure in young children. The sense of something lacking, of constriction, that the children bring back from sleep, along with an unconscious expectation of encountering goodness, is taken away when they experience goodness in the bodily care given them. They gradually develop confidence that the losses they suffered at birth, as in expulsion from the womb can be made up for by the affection and care of others.

The first such consideration is a replacing of a child's lost prenatal home by helping it to feel at home in its body. That is possible only when the way a child is cared for allows him to experience a resonating memory of his lost home. And that is the deeper secret of the life sense. If it develops in a healthy manner, this continually soothes the longing/awakening feeling of constriction and loss that is otherwise relieved only in sleep. The reason for this is that the life sense functions not merely as a perceptive organ for bodily conditions, as it is very generally described, but as a carrier of messages, telling of experiences of goodness and shelter, woven into the etheric or life body.

Education and self-education – tolerance

Parents are the ones who saturate a child's vital organism with loving kindness, and in so doing create a milieu for the life sense in which she can find herself. But that is something you cannot do alone; the child's angel is cooperating with you from the other side. Through the angel's doing, children respond to their parents' efforts with unlimited readiness to receive and to reciprocate evidence of love, and, in a playfully imitative way, to take on the mood of caring, comforting, and a protective concern for other weaker creatures. Over and beyond this, children's angels are responsible for adapting their organisms relatively quickly to earthly conditions that, to begin with, were so alien to them. It can be expresses thus: By night the child experiences goodness in a bodily way from within as a result of the angel's energizing, harmonizing help, thus supporting the developmental maturation, not just of the child's organs, but of its life sense as well. By day, parents aid this work of the angel with caring and solicitous actions.

But what does all this have to do with moral education and social adequacy? For what capacities of this nature is the life sense laying a foundation?

The answer is apparent in everything that has been discussed thus far: it is the life sense as the prerequisite for inner peace, for harmony, for sensing oneself as complete and at one with oneself. As the sense, too, that makes one's body the bearer of memories of goodness and shelter, it enables one to surrender oneself to contemplative soul moods such as unhurried peacefulness, reverence, reflection. We have to be at peace in ourselves in order to listen and to have the patience to open ourselves with anticipatory interest to people or events. These three qualities and strengths flourish in the nurturing ground of the life sense.

We are speaking here of the same capacities or attitudes that we found essential to educators if they are to work in the right way on a child's life sense. There is a pedagogical law to be discovered here, namely, that that sense is best served by an educational application of inner capacities that we ourselves have developed as the fruit of nurturing our own life sense. The same law applies to all the other basic senses. What always works wholesomely on the body-based orientation that is a child's primary characteristic is the corresponding characteristic metamorphosed into a soul quality in caretaking adults. We can, therefore, not expect our children to become instantly patient, reverential, and kind from seeing us behave in that manner. That would be most mistaken as well as harmful, for wrong expectations have consequences. But we help thereby to create a foundation on which children not only can but want to develop the inner attitudes that they currently experience in you and through you as eminently confidence-inspiring and security-enhancing.

This helps us to answer the question of what future moral capacities we and the children's angels need to consider in relation to the life sense. Reverence, unhurried peacefulness, attentive expectation, patience—all weigh equally in importance in human intercourse. It is possible to listen to and understand others in their individual difference, to accept them as they are, and take real interest in them, only if we stand firmly on our own ground while meeting them with the inner collectedness and circumspection of a confident life sense orientation that has been built into our personality structure. I emphasize that this sense appears on a higher level as a sense of biographical identity and continuity, in other words as firmly structured self-awareness. This latter soul quality is essential to the acquiring of the above capacities, all of which require a certain degree of selflessness. We can forget ourselves only when we are firmly self-grounded; otherwise, self-forgetting begets fear, fear that impels us reputedly to attempt to get back to ourselves in a hurried and intolerant mood, seeking refuge in our accustomed opinions and prejudices, sympathies, and antipathies. Self-groundness helps us avoid the feeling that the proper boundary between ourselves and others is not being preserved. (This is a psychological fact that spiritual schools that attach too little value to the ego completely ignore.) I repeat: only a firmly established self-awareness makes genuine self-forgetting possible.

If we now look for an inclusive term for the social qualities we have been discussing, what can we find that sums them all up?

It seems to me that the concept "active tolerance" best serves us. Active tolerance means not only leaving others free to be themselves in all their individual differences, while taking a gentle and unprejudiced interest in them, but really wanting to understand them sufficiently to honor their ways of being and behaving without judging them by one's own standard.

This is a capacity so rare today that it can almost be said that every one of us is suffering the consequences of a disturbance of our life sense! How painfully we have to labor, in tiresome efforts at self-discipline, to acquire the virtue of tolerance, once its importance has been recognized! If the "open secret" of the life sense were to be widely enough discussed and practically applied as a matter of course to educational directives, we would be laying at least the tendency to cultivate tolerance in every baby's cradle. Later on, we will see of course that more than a favorable life sense orientation is needed to develop true interest in our fellow human beings. But the interest, the understanding participation that is the inner aspect of tolerance, is a product of the life sense.

So our finding is that the life sense is the prerequisite for the later development of unhurried peacefulness, reverence, and patience, which gives birth in the social realm to the virtue of active tolerance. This, in turn, enables us to truly honor and accept our fellow humans in their unique individual being.

Let us keep in mind that angels are concerned with implanting the "organic peace" over which the life sense stands guard and through which confidence in life is rayed upward into the soul the capacities of reverence and patience, in order that the basic social virtue, active tolerance, evolves from them. We help angels to accomplish this by taking into account the fact that children in their first years of life need, above all, to develop trust in their bodies. Everything we do in this respect should make palpable that reverence, patience, and goodness are a foreshadowing of future achievements. We can trust here the young children's imitative learning to bring forth these qualities.

If you have a markedly excitable and nervous child, actively create an internal image of the child along with an undisguised plea for help and take this into sleep with you. You will experience a change gradually taking place within you in the sense that it will become easier to translate your insights into actions. That evidence of a new state of affairs developing which was earlier referred to as "fingertip sensitivity," will make its appearance. It might also be called an instinct for doing the right thing at the right time with an inner certainty that communicates itself to the child.

The case of an excitable, nervous child is most clearly defined as one in which, at some point, contact with his angel has been broken off or injured. This injury occurred at the point where the angel was attempting to prepare the soul out of which would be born the capacities for reverence and patience that re-open most fully in the virtue of tolerance. It is with respect to these that the angel has come into insufficient contact with the child. That can result from many causes; the adults involved are not necessarily to blame. However, it is important to realize that they can contribute to healing the child-angel relationship at the point in question. And one aspect is, that in addition to the other means suggested, we train ourselves to strengthen/develop the specific soul-capacities in which the child is having a hard time to come to rights: patience, reverence, and unhurried peacefulness; they are the ones needed in our dealings with children whose life sense has suffered ensuing deprivation.

You need to work on your tolerance, too—the angels' goal is to nurture a mature life sense. Anyone living with an uneasy spirit will not question this. If tolerance is in too short supply (I mean, particularly, tolerance in meeting the challenges that surface in daily life with such children), nothing works. It may sound paradoxical, but healing anothers' damaged life sense depends first of all on being tolerant oneself—for how do you expect to produce patience and reverence if you are upset all day long and run around with the feeling that your child ought to be different than he or she is?

The first need of all is to accept such a troubled child as the troubled child he or she is; the rest follows. We are our angel's acceptable partners only if our motives as educators are not self-serving. You cannot be concerned for your reputation as a "good parent," showcasing your child as a successful product. Nor should you try to get rid of the eternal bother, but rather make it your sole aim to keep the child from suffering, to spare him all foreseeable difficulties and shortcomings.

This requirement applies, of course, to educating in general, but it is particularly important in the case of troubled children. They should be made to feel that the help given them springs from the adult's thoroughgoing acceptance—from a completely tolerant attitude.

3.

A STUDY OF THE SENSE OF TOUCH

THE SKIN AS A SENSE ORGAN

Let us go on now further to the basal senses and to the developmental problems related to them.

First, let us consider the sense of touch and ask again what social or—we may say—religious impulses children's angels want to implant in them as seeds for the future as they help in developing the sense of touch.

What is the nature of this participation? What problems surface if a child's contract with her angel is impaired at this point?

Let us be clear here that the sense of touch involves much more than the hands' capacity to feel whether an object is soft or hard, rough or smooth. That is only a small part of it. We need to ask what makes it possible in the first place for our hands to derive information about something from the nature of its surface. And the most obvious answer is, "Why, because we have feeling in our hands."

But that is a vague sort of answer. Where, exactly, is the feeling capacity referred to?

It is in our skin! And it is not only our hands that our skin encloses; we are enclosed by skin over our whole body. Our capacity to feel with our fingertips is shared in principle by every part of us, by some areas even more intensely. You have surely had the experience of holding something in your hand that felt so pleasant that you wanted to intensify the feeling. So you probably lifted the object to your cheek or neck and stroked it gently. The cheeks and the neck are body parts extremely sensitive to touch, as are the tongue and lips, the insides of the thighs, and the section of the back between the shoulder blades. In short, the skin covering the whole surface of the body is the organ whereby the sense of touch perceives. Some portions of it are more sensitive than others. But on the whole, the total bodily surface is the source of our experience of touch, and it does this uninterruptedly. When we bathe, we have the sense of water touching us all over, and the same holds true when wind blows over us. We have a day long touch-sensing of the clothes we are wearing, of the ground we stand on or walk over, of the elbows we land on, of the back when we lean against a wall. We have an uninterrupted experience of touch on the part of the tongue and teeth and palate all the time we are speaking and even of the eyelids when we blink. You will notice all this if you pay attention, for every phase of life teems with touch experiences.

We can hardly imagine how we would feel if the sense of touch were suddenly shut off; it would certainly involve an extensive loss of orientation. But try imagining this anyhow. Take hold of some object you cannot feel, shake hands; eat some food; distinguish between liquids and solids in your month, or sense the texture of the ground under your feet.

We cannot really imagine how any of this world feels, nor have we considered in the least what weight or consequences would follow in the event of such a loss.

CHARACTERISTICS OF TOUCH PERCEPTION

First, here are two important "marginal notes." We raised the question as to how it is that our hands—or, more precisely, our skin—are able to identify objects or substances. This is due to the fact the whole surface of the human body is an exceptionally sensitive perceptive organ, since our skin conveys feeling.

But there is something that needs to be taken into account here. If, standing in a totally dark place, I touch an object that is round and cool and smooth, but not completely hard, and I realize that the object is an apple, a lot has gone on in the fraction of a second between the first touch sensation and the conclusion, "Ahh! It's an apple." This is a sequence of events that has nothing directly to do with a pure experience of touch.

That will be clear to you if you now review the situation in the completely dark place with the assumption that you have never primarily seen or held an apple and that an apple is a totally unfamiliar thing in your experience. In such a case, no amount of handling it would help you to identify it as an apple. But that is not the whole story. You feel this unfamiliar object all over and come up with the fact that it is round, dented in at the top, mostly smooth, but at some places scaly, and so on. These are quite active findings.

Now, is it the sense of touch that makes these findings?

No, obviously not. Impressions conveyed by the sense of touch gave rise to the findings, but the process of assigning qualities is itself not part of the touch experience; rather, it is an act of consciousness added onto the experience of touch. It is only because you grasp connections, relating similar experiences to one another as you draw on a treasury of memories—in short, you are able to enrich perceiving with thinking—that you find it possible to attach a series of touch impressions to an object as its characteristics.

Rudolf Steiner went so far as to say that "exactly stated, we ascribe characteristics of the sense of touch to objects (perceived)." In other words, we have a touch impression, and we experience it in ourselves as a result of coming into contact with the thing touched. We experience it as a bodily event shared on a soul level as well. We note a change in our inner state and "project this back into external space" (Steiner). That is the second thing to observe. Again Steiner observes, "Our skin comes in contact with some object. What happens to bring about perception of the object we touch takes place, of course, within the skin, within the body. Thus, the process of touching is one that goes on inside us." Put another way, touch perception is an internal resonating in response to direct contact with an external physical world. We ascertain, by means of our sense of touch first, the coming into contact with, the striking against the external world of matter that makes us aware of a boundary. Secondly, in the subtler aspect of the process, the whole body reacts as a resonator to the various means of the touching, and our soul shares in experiencing the "vibrations" that travel through our organisms in ways that differ in accordance with the rough or smooth, sharp or blunt, hard or soft impressions received. It is important, for an understanding of the touch sense, to keep in mind the fact that soul life participates in physiological changes. Corresponding impressions are seized upon by our consciousness in the way described and rayed back to the objects in external space. When we touch something (and the subtler the sensation is, the truer this is), our souls hearken to the music played by the outer world on our bodily instrument. Coarse contacts call forth hollow-sounding chords, or, if they are displeasing or actually painful, they are experienced as shrill discords. Pleasing contacts pursue their way inward with beneficent effects. But sensitivity is not a boon in cases when the things we touch lack character. Objects made of plastic give rise to neither pleasant nor unpleasant vibrations. Instead, our souls experience nonfeeling in the form of an oppressive emptiness. One is reminded of listening expectantly while plucking a harp string and hearing nothing! The experience is, of course, different when you touch them as opposed to hearing a tone, but it is, nevertheless, keenly felt.

I want to reassure parents that the above is not meant as a dogmatic back-to-nature exhortation. There are many excellent environmental reasons for manufacturing artificial materials. We cannot, for example, go on endlessly decimating our forest resources in preference for wood. There are complex issues here, and we gain nothing from a fundamentalist approach. But plastics really have no place in children's rooms. A fundamentalism of sorts is justified here. If you force a child to live with flickering fluorescent lighting, it will not be long before he develops visual problems. And when children are given a majority of plastic toys and wear clothing made of artificial materials, they are subjected not only to early injury to their sense of touch, but also to their life sense as well. These two senses are closely interwoven, as can be seen from what has previously been noted as changes effected in the bodily state by touch-experiences. You will remember that the life senses' secondary function is its perception of just such changes occurring in a sensed state-of-being.

God sensing

We realize how extremely important it is for children to have a sufficient chance to develop their sense of touch through handling natural materials. Rudolf Steiner pointed out that the subtle touch perception characterized above as *body-soul resonating* has two aspects. We have already explored one aspect as the sensing of the manifold nuances of skin contact with the external world that enables us to have intimate experience of the range of phenomena in the surrounding world. This is the origin of our capacity to characterize objects and to confirm the existence of a world of material objects systematized under various qualitative headings.

Something very fundamental takes place in touch perception. "What the sense of touch conveys in sensations of roughness and smoothness, hardness and softness, radiates outward," says Steiner. This aspect has already been discussed. But he characterizes the ultimate primal phenomenon, the "denominator" of the whole range of touch impressions as "streaming inward and remaining wholly unconscious." "The sensation of touch is like being suffused by the universal substantiality of the cosmos, of being permeated by being-ness as such." If I understand him rightly, he is speaking here of the hidden aspect of the phenomenon of matter. We are aware of the existence of an external material world only because our nerve-sense system is so organized that though we feel related as individual existences to all other existing things and creatures, we sense our separation from them. The external aspect of the phenomenon called "matter" is our touch-conveyed sensing of our own boundedness, which alone enables us to "ascertain the existence of an external world" (Steiner). I am on one side of the border; everything else is on the other side. And our skins are the focus where what is other touches me. The external world is perceived by the touch sense.

That is the explanation of the I-world schism, of dual consciousness as awareness of my apartness from the rest of creation. The outer world has reality for me only because I am separated from it, made aware of this by my existence as a self in a body.

All further soul and spiritual advances in autonomy are possible only on this basis; it enables that touch sense to ascertain/confirm the existence of an external material and alien world that we keep at bay in order to assert ourselves as separate entities with a life of our own. That is the outer aspect of the phenomenon "matter": we experience our difference from the rest of creation.

But there exists, too, the aforementioned hidden aspect of feeling, whereby we overcome the separateness, even though it does not disappear entirely. Rudolf Steiner tells us, "With every experience of touch there rays into the soul a feeling profoundly stirred by the creative power that underlies all material existence and accounts for the wide range of differentiation in the phenomenal universe." We might speak here of a primordial substantiality existing before creation and accounting for "everything made that can be made," a substantiality "that suffices everything, including ourselves, and also sustains us."

In the end, Rudolf Steiner calls this "the all-permeating God-substance" and characterizes the sense and supersensible experience of it as "being suffused with the sensing of God." We should try to conceive this as simply as possible and not allow ourselves to be disturbed by his unaccustomed choice of words to describe it. If we explore the world with a subtle sense of touch we have not only the single experience of a boundary, nor, merely, the differentiated substantial impressions of perceptions of sound. Beyond these impressions is an immediate encounter, taking place on a deeply hidden level, with the very ground of our existence. There we come in contact with the reality that lies at the foundation of all realized single phenomena, the realm Jean Paul Sartre calls "L'etant" (where things are in their primal state). Allow me to remark that what he had in mind was "the nothing—in the heart of being," whereas Rudolf Steiner, in his scientific investigation of the senses rather than as a philosophical explorer, came up with exactly the opposite finding; he described an encounter with "the state of being as such" at the heart of all transitory, externally perceived, supposed existence.

It would be possible to refute Sartre's empty-ended metaphysics on the basis of a subtle grasp of the phenomenon of touch. I am of the general opinion that no such thing as fruitful philosophizing is at all possible any more without recourse to a spiritual psychological approach to perception and will.

THE SENSE OF TOUCH AND INTEREST IN THE WORLD: DISSONANCE, RESONANCE, EVIDENCE

On the one hand, we can describe the sense of touch from the perspective where, "we come into continuous crudest contact with the external world" (Steiner), and this works, as we have seen, on a hidden level; on the other hand, we can experience touch as the sense that brings us into the most direct touch with the spiritual inscribed into matter. That element can be inwardly experienced by us to the degree that our sense of touch has matured into a perceptive tool whereby we not only contact the world of external objects but explore it further in its differentiation and material makeup. We do so in ways that allow us to speak of our findings as evidence, that is, "as completely certain."

This is a certainty not achievable by thinking. Thinking, as has been pointed out, cannot alone supply any kind of certainty. Quite the opposite, in fact. The nature of things can only be grasped by thinking when an actual ascertaining of reality has taken place at deeper soul levels. And if we ask how that comes about, we have first to take into account what has been discussed here as the three aspects of world exploration served by touch, referred to and summed up here for clarity's sake as:

1) an experiencing of boundaries or difference (object-awareness),

2) resonance (a calling forth of sensations through bodily co-vibrating, which we refer back to objects as their distinctive attributes), and

3) evidence (becoming aware of the state of "being" or "existence" as such).

The three sequences here correspond to the depth of the experience. In its totality it takes place within us and beneath the conscious level. But the experience of differences occurs at the periphery, of resonance alternating between outside and inside, of evidence ("God sensing") at a wholly hidden level.

Our living thinking is able to lay hold on sense-transmitted reality only because the phenomenal world, first experienced as outside us, is brought by the sense of touch to profoundly inner participatory experience. Put another way: our skin, insofar as we experience it as both a sheath and a boundary, not only constitutes part of the outer world for our consciousness, but serves as our subtlest perceptive organ for that world. We would have no relationship to reality if we lacked the assurance that touch gives us that we exist! We would fall into wild confusion as to what is inside us and what outside, just as very young children do before their sense of touch matures. We could neither form concepts nor enter into communication of any kind, for the former requires distancing ourselves in the act of observation, while the latter takes place as an active establishing of connection where it was previously lacking. The act of touching is the prototype of all the deeds that connect us with and establish our understanding of everything other than ourselves, the basic gesture in all learning. Touching means identifying the other as other in direct confrontation while simultaneously carefully exploring its nature and uniqueness.

We refer here, of course, to the intentional or willed aspect of touching. "Interest" or participatory attention best describes the attitude our consciousness experiences in such acts. At such moments we can say that the activity of the touch sense is that of a tutor outside his own field.

One could say that genuine interest is a controlled, sublimated (because it is raised to a higher level), subtler touch impulse. That needs to be kept firmly in mind.

THE STUDY OF THE HUMAN BEING AND EDUCATIONAL PRACTICE

It would be understandable if you were now feeling that I had overloaded you with theoretical ballast. But I assure you that educational practice benefits in many ways from exploring the function of the touch sense more thoroughly than is usually done.

We should be familiar by now with detailed reasons for certain groups' reiterated urging that children's sense of touch be given thorough nurturing. But can we be sure that there is anything more to this advice than, for example, advising washing their hands before eating?

Matters of this sort need to have their full import recognized. To regard nurturing the basal senses as a matter of mere social or psychological significance is to underrate their significance. Lots of people have on some occasion read or heard all too popular discussions of this theme and concluded that overall care of the body is of great importance for children's sense of well-being and peer acceptance. That is right, of course. But it has as little to do with the problem of the bodily senses as a shirt collar's cleanliness has to do with relieving swallowing difficulties. I have already pointed out in connection with the life sense that it serves no purpose to do a professional cleaner's job on a child as though in keeping with the motto, "First wash the kitchen floor, then the sink, and finally the toilet." A skin which is shining clean in every pore is by no means a well-developed touch-sense. What we are discussing here goes far deeper, and when deeper matters are superficially interpreted, facts are falsified. To give you just "a feeling" for them or to treat you as though you were incapable of clear thinking is, in effect, to declare you incompetent. But it is the parents who carry the main educational responsibility, and I consider it ruinous to keep continually involved people unaware of the educational processes needed in their job—or what is just as bad, to shun the effort of making these clear and just hand out recipes instead.

In my consultations, I am consistently impressed with how important it is to give useful advice to parents in the form of mostly practical, regularly repeated acts and exercises, based on anthropological findings. This creates the transparency needed, so that what has to be done at home is carried out with insight. That takes time, consciousness, and effort for all concerned. But it is worth it, as we see by the fact that the better these practices and exercises are understood, the more disciplined will be the manner of their being carried out.

It can also be noted that when parents deepened their understanding of the way they looked at things and accepted the suggestions made, it usually happened shortly thereafter that they returned to appointments with me saying that they felt the advice given them simply confirmed their own conclusions.

With respect to the touch sense, those who are the primary child-nurturers need first to understand its connection with the summing up concepts "difference, resonance, evidence"— in other words, its importance for an experienced certainty of existence and reality, for a capacity to make qualitative judgments and achieve conceptual energy. Secondly, they need to know that interest, as a questioning, marveling soul approach, is a sublimated touch impulse.

Taking all this into account, we begin to see what the real reason for nurturing the touch sense is, what the child's angel's purpose is in working from the other, the nightside, to form the "receptacle of the touch sense"—the sense that we may justly characterize as the "sense of reality."

What social capacity, what common feeling should be developed to fill that receptacle? What are the educational skills needed for recognizing and dealing helpfully with touch sense developmental problems?

WHAT DOES "UNDERSTANDING" MEAN?

Allow me, before addressing this question concretely, to make a few side comments on my previous finding that the touch sense lays the groundwork for our ability to grasp physical sensory reality in living thinking.

You must have noticed that I used the term "living" thinking. That does not mean the kind of logic that demands objectivity and impersonality of the type natural science and scientifically orientated philosophy have fostered, which is worthy of deepest respect, though it often uses Beelzebub to drive out the devil. Granted that even where efforts to achieve a spiritual world outlook are concerned, they can only benefit from being subjected to a disciplining that rejects personal likes and dislikes. Unless one reaffirms the phenomena as a matter of direct experience, then even further extrapolating thinking (though avoiding the pitfall of basing itself on confused and emotional "opinions") falls into something so unreal as to be the ghostly death zone of lifeless, soulless, intellectuality. It plays a very considerable role there in judging natural phenomena, as these present themselves to our senses, because it is thought that no subjective perception of any kind can contribute to the discovery of fact.

This view fails to note that there are subjectively mediated approaches to objectivity—a realm of universally recognized facts that can be entered only through the door of personal experience. Every molecular biologist, every astrophysicist ought to be held in a way comparable to a psychiatrist's training by self-observation, by doing regular exercises in perception based on Goethe's color theory, or by subjecting themselves to Hugo Kukelhaus' method of sense-training. This would provide a guarantee that research done in laboratories or on computers would receive necessary supplementation in a deepening or enhancing of perceptive capacities able to convey information as to how phenomena appear to direct human experience. That would bring home the fact that the language these phenomena speak has only a single set of "grammatical" laws.

Nowadays, the findings of laboratory analysis and experimentation are always considered more important than any arrived at by smelling, listening, tasting, seeing, or touching, and digital reckoning is held more significant than any discoveries made on the basis of an ability to understand things by feeling one's way sensitively into them. That is why we are living in a world in which art and a fund of ideas derived from wide-awake observation of life-living processes in nature and human society, and applied to the solving of pressing problems, remain so troublingly underdeveloped, despite tremendous advances in technology and the huge accumulation of information. We have lost awareness of the fact that instead of withdrawing to "strategic positions," observers can profit from becoming personally involved and affected. Keeping at a cool distance is not always the best source of learning, nor is close proximity invariably "unscientific." On the contrary, there is a species of relationship to reality that can be brought about only when a person striving for insight includes personal concern in his or her approach to the matter studied. Anyone desirous of understanding the "language" of phenomena has a vital interest in their most immediate state of being. That person wants to approach them for a revelation of their being, and that involves honoring their innate intrinsic worth.

Yes, indeed! Tree trunks, crystals, wind, water—all have innate intrinsic worth that can be experienced! And there is no way of getting to know anything existing outside oneself that so clearly conveys an experience of that worth as attentively touching contact, as listening to the feelings generated by touching. All other relating in which the search for insight is combined with a personally concerned approach is an offshoot of the touch experience. I will not ask you to bear with me in the sort of hand-wringing complaint about science heard today from every superficial quarter. But we cannot escape recognizing that a tragic waste of capacities of consciousness is going on, capacities originating in the experience of touch. That is an alarming symptom. What must be relearned is an eye for creation, taught by the most basic, primal touch-experience, with an interested eye such as we have been discussing. This way of seeing does not dissect things as though they were trophies of a hunt. It rests upon them with sensitive reserve, putting its questioning without trying to squeeze out answers, and with no other object then to understand.

A LOVING RELATIONSHIP TOWARD THE WORLD

"Touching is an experience in which one's inner being reacts to an external process in a way no other sense experience conveys," says Rudolf Steiner. That is why "we would have no feeling for God if we didn't possess a sense of touch." We have a profoundly inner experience of the outer world in touching it, and this alone enables us to contact it with understanding, for touching is the basis of the certainty we feel that something really exists.

Rudolf Steiner calls this certainty "God sensing," the sense of being permeated by "the God substance." What a mystery it is that the sense, on the one hand, brings us "in the crudest manner" into contact with the outer world, and, on the other hand, conveys such far-from-crude evidence, and moreover, plays such an important role in our ability to live "with understanding" into the innate quality of things.

Take, for example, a process wherein we characterize the thing touched as "rough," call our pressure on it "hard," describe the contact as "abrading," and identify the object as tree bark.

We note here that even leaving out eye and nose sensations, something more was involved than an experience of touch. We need to include the sense of balance for ascertaining pressure, the sense of motion for ascertaining the nature of the contact. These will be themes of later discussion. The life sense, in its secondary function, indicates changes in the inner state of being registered on the scale of well-being or lack of it. Furthermore, conceptual thinking based on experience is essential to "evaluating" the process. But none of this lessens the central importance of the sense of touch in the overall event, first identified by touching as "contact with the outside world" and then experienced in the above-described phenomenon of resonance in so nuanced a manner that making qualitative findings becomes possible. Many things play a role here, as stated, but the touch sense is the guarantor of a differentiated concept of reality. The example of the "hard abrasion" lets us see clearly what might be called a further law abidingness, in that the harder the contact, the more impressive is the experiencing of boundaries in touching. This is the aspect of "difference," which can be stretched to the point of rejection, in which the whole individual reacts with soul and body; the senses of balance, motion, and life are all involved in the irritation. The more delicate the contact, the more the resonance aspect predominates. We open ourselves to the impression, bringing about an involvement, an inclusion of the life sense and the senses of motion and balance. This results in a harmonious concord of all the basal senses, which we might describe as a state of "preconscious interest." And in this case, if contact is gentle and caring and, therefore, favors "lingering dwelling" in it, the consequent conscious forming of judgment sets in a far less divided manner than it can after hefty or perhaps even painful contact.

The above is a very abridged presentation, but the observations on which it is based are extremely significant for the development of the touch sense in children. Caring, lingering skin contact, based on participating attentiveness, is essential to the later development of a healthy power of judgment and establishes confidence in existence. "God sensing" flourishes in the soul's uttermost depths where resonance, which is inner vibratory response, predominates, rather than the experience of a set boundary relieving what psychology sees as an agonizing "uncertainty of existing" cropping up particularly in younger years. ("Am I really here at all? Is anyone or anything else really there?") This doubt can increase to the point of illness unless the sense of touch is well-developed.

Let us state it quite clearly. A loving relationship toward the world, finding its nurture in the sense of touch, is the means of overcoming the existential doubt we are all naturally familiar with. And we will all agree that there is nothing passive about love; it always contains an active element, be it ever so concealed or deeply inward. The more deeply an impression touches without overwhelming us as perceiving subjects (which the sense of touch also provides for by the boundaries it sets up, protecting us against too great a flood of external impressions), the more we naturally incline to a caring approach. Crude, insensitive behavior is always the sign of a lack of fine feeling. The term "fingertip sensitivity" is also used to denote the same thing.

A lack of either can be paid to various causes. Those who approach objects or follow creatures with indifference or self-interested curiosity behave with as little fine feeling as those who lose their boundary in falling all over themselves in response to some attraction exerted from outside. That is one way in which perceiving subjects are overwhelmed by impressions. The perceiver is not under his own control; sympathy makes him act like the proverbial bull in a china shop. Another way, familiar to all of us, is that of over impressionability that sparks automatic rejection as a boundary-emphasizing reaction. Here, too, the purpose is to lessen the sensitivity of fine feeling. We encapsulate ourselves in an instinctive effort to keep something at bay. This theme has been fully dealt with in my book, *The Riddle of Fear*.

The sense of touch has the task of bringing about a healthy, mobile balance between too great and too little impressionability, between openness and boundedness, between sympathy and antipathy. When it is well-developed, its metamorphosed functioning as the regulator of a soul/spiritual relationship to the world makes it possible for an unthreatened selfhood to take profoundly participating interest in what surrounds it. If this fact is taken sufficiently into account in education, especially in the early years, children's angels are provided with a "vessel" into which to pour, in later years, what could be called thoughtful caring for others, tenderness, and consideration. We have analyzed interest, in its feeling aspect, as caring concern; that is genuine interest's most basic, naturally indwelling element. This, you will agree, is a lofty social capacity first practiced in contact with the material environment, but it reaches ultimate refinement in the social attitude described as the grace of brotherly feeling.

Just as the life sense lays the foundation of the community-building capacity of tolerance, what begins as the ascertainment of reality by means of touch is the seed-source of caring concern in our approach to life. Moral instruction cannot hold a candle to it, for we have to have an ability to grasp what lives in the world as morality—and I refer here not to postulates, but to living morality. This ability is composed of elements of which we first gain basic knowledge by means of our self-perceiving body-related senses. Although these senses primarily convey perception of our own bodily states, they are to a considerable degree responsible for regulating our relationships to what is around us. This is a fact often overlooked or else insufficiently emphasized.

The imitative readiness of a child's soul to love the good, in which the presence of her "higher self," the angel, makes itself known, comes to expression in the realm of touch in the child's awakening to feelings of gratitude and confidence. The tender care she has received awakens capacities which can later be transformed into social impulses. Children experience such tenderness as a bodily impression that justifies an expectation felt by them. Completeness comes of it. As they awaken from the security of sleep where angels do their work, children turn to us with a questioning to which they receive a deeply satisfying answer if, in our care of them (in the way we convey a sense of their dignity as bodily beings), we give them a protected feeling and an experience of gentleness coming from outside, in the way we touch them. We are their first experience of an "outside"; we are its representatives. It is our job to make them aware that contact with reality, which has unavoidably painful aspects for every child, can be beneficial as well. That is a basic confidence-building experience literally "felt by the skin." A healthy sense of existence is needed for the development of social capacities. A person always living in fear of closeness as a painful experience cannot make friends with others, because that means closeness and consequent vulnerability.

Here again we see how extraordinarily interlaced the various aspects of human development are. Discussion of moral education has to include mention of emotional and will development, and this is in turn closely allied to the maturity of the senses that is our major focal topic in today's deliberation.

THE SPATIALLY-BOUNDED BODILY SELF

The statement was made that angels do their work by night. The strengthening and ordering with which they reinforce and regulate children's work on their own metabolic processes nurtures the life sense. We have to do our part in this by approaching them in a patient, reverential mood that calms and warms and supports the rhythmic element, thus fostering a sense of bodily well-being. Everything else we do around them in that mood, rather than in a hectic, superficial manner, is imitatively absorbed and works harmoniously on their organisms.

We saw that it is just those wiggleworms, the type of child who has problems in this area, who most especially need to be handled with tolerance. It is not a matter of wish-washy letting-things-be, but of genuine bearing-with-them. There is a vast difference between the two attitudes. These children need consistent, consequential treatment, but we must not make the mistake of always resenting the nature they were born with. They are particularly dependent on our regard for them, which must be made the cornerstone of the help given them in their upbringing. That holds true even when, at times, such "help" is not welcome and is experienced as restrictions that have to be accepted. What is particularly needed here is a lively pedagogical tolerance, the product of the educator's self-education. And in this connection I cite again the words that should become our motto: "It is invariably those qualities raised by adults to soul capacities that work curatively on the same primary, but bodily-oriented qualities, in children."

Now what is the situation with regard to the sense of touch?

Just as children's angels work on the bodily processes in a strengthening and ordering manner to develop the life sense, their work on the touch sense could be described as "forming and configuring." Shaping forces are actively molding a child's body, particularly in sleep, for by day these forces are more or less used up and need to be night-regenerated. They are the forces that gradually form within young growing bodies. They carry out "the architectural plan of creation." They may also be thanked for the bodily image we have of ourselves in a sure feeling for our bodily proportions, for their size and spatial extension. In Rudolf Steiner's book, *Anthroposophy, A Fragment,* he gives a provisional sketch of his sense doctrine; he writes that the life sense endows us with our experience of ourselves as "bodily selves occupying space." Applying a variation of this to the sense of touch, we can say that it enables us to experience ourselves as bodily selves with spatial boundaries. That experience is the source of the above-described sensation we have of being enclosed in a sheath, which we owe to the processes taking place unconsciously in sleep. Anyone who has had to stay awake several nights in a row is only too familiar with the adverse effects on his or her sensing of a sheath. One of the first such efforts is one's incapacity to make a correct estimate of how much space one's body takes up, where its boundaries lie, with the result that one is constantly bumping into things, misjudging distances, feeling certain bodily areas swollen, and so on. One becomes utterly clumsy. It is not just the indistinct body image that accounts for this. The senses of movement and balance are upset too, but it is bodily orientation, the sense of bodily form and extension, that chiefly suffers.

It is well known that lack of sleep also causes emotional oversensitivity. Everything "rubs us raw." We feel jumpy, fussy, and under attack. Sense impressions, particularly noises, are hard to bear. We all know the hysterical state we can get into. The reason for it is our loss of sheathing that makes its appearance on the soul level when our bodily image becomes indistinct. This condition is popularly described as "thin-skinned," for the sense organ of the skin in which we feel ourselves clothed has become threadbare. The feeling aspect has overbalanced the orientating bodily image, the being-sheathed sensation.

This provides a clue for all sense research. All sense functions have both a soul feeling and a bodily orientating aspect, and they should receive equal attention from investigators.

ARRIVAL ON THE EARTH

If we adults live more or less healthy lives and are not exposed to extreme pressures, we should have achieved some degree of stability; we would otherwise not be able to manage what our days bring us.

But it is important to realize that we are not born with a clear awareness of our bodies. Young children have not as yet a conscious experience of their bodily bounds, and, therefore, of their enclosing sheaths. That develops only very gradually and because their sensing of it is so vague at first, they are easily frightened. A lot of nonsense is talked and written about this. I have recently read that fear is something acquired only with the passage of time. A child's book I read keeps saying that the five-year-old in the story still lives blissfully in a sunny world, with the harsh experience of fear yet to be encountered. This is typical adult nonsense! Another book, a psychological text, actually asserts that the best care for fear-plagued grownups is to recall their state of mind in early childhood, since that was a time of life completely devoid of fear! Mistaken views of this kind come from romanticizing childhood instead of observing the actual facts. The latter course reveals that fear, as part of the human condition, is there from the beginning, and in potent measure.

The baby's expulsion from the mother's body is immediately sensed as a being tossed out into a sea of fear. People who speak of a general birth trauma to which all newborns are subject are indeed looking more realistically at the facts than those who make up stories of early childhood's blissful "unity with the whole world" and the like. The latter states only a partial truth that leads astray. The more important fact is that young children are still deeply connected with the spiritual world, so much so that they are actually constantly trying to get back to it. Parents ought to give themselves over to the illusion that their precious presence is a newborn's dearest joy. It may be that on earth, if a tiny person could speak, it would be telling us, "You are dear and precious and I decided to come to you. But there is another scene of peace and shelter; the time I'm allowed to spend there grows shorter and shorter, and you can't make up to me for its loss. Leaving it was hard for me, though I left it only at my own deepest prompting and prepared myself thoroughly to do so. It will take a long time to get used to the change." That is about what we would be hearing.

That is the deeper reason why infants want to spend all their time sleeping. And I am saying "want to," not "must." Of course, necessity is part of it, but more important is the deep longing felt. In the case of newborn infants, sleeping means being at home. They are not yet at home with us on the earth. The earth is a foreign landscape; they have gradually to grow familiar with it. The very core of our job as educators is to help them achieve this.

"To grow familiar with" is only another way of saying "overcoming fear." Every time a child falls asleep it turns itself over to its angel and experiences primal protectedness, the sheathed state. And on every such occasion the angel needs infinite patience to persuade the child that it has to go back again to that alien land, that it cannot have everything at once: beloved parents, the earthly pleasures and delights it has gradually been learning to appreciate, the many exciting new experiences, and still enjoy the timeless, carefree, unburdened life of heavenly existence.

Yes, these little new arrivals are pretty demanding; that is why they cry at every excuse. It ought to be clear to us that they were used to better things in the place they came from. If this strikes us, we are all-to-humanly torn between a desire to spoil them or a natural annoyance at their expressed "egoism."

It is not egoism at all, of course, but simply a problem of making the necessary adjustments. If, instead of spoiling, we give babies sensible loving care and transform our annoyance at the supposed egoism into a style of training that demonstrates balanced ability to make sacrifices and to face up to unpleasantness, we are on the right track.

It is certainly essential to have a sense of humor in dealing with these little princes and princesses. They are manifestly accustomed to giving orders; they behave as though they came from a realm where, as a matter of course, their every wish was read from their eyes (and that is actually the case in certain respects). But we should never forget that we are witnessing real needs that we are charged with meeting.

This aspect should not be overemphasized, however. There is the other side, where we witness children's joy in life, their enthusiastic storming into the world, their stunned amazement at its wonders. But laying a firm foundation for this outcome means preparing a suitable reception for them here on earth and helping them in their early years to develop trust in their strange new environment—in short, to overcome their fear.

In undertaking this, we can count on a child's indestructible, unaffrighted core, which returns from sleep ever freshly laden with confidence and trust. I refer to that core of his being that holds body and soul together. From it proceeds by day what the child's angel has built into him during sleep as strengthening, ordering, formative impulses. We can confirm this from our own observation if we have fostered the bodily senses that Christoph Lindenberg describes as "mediating feelings of security and existence."

EDUCATION AND SELF-EDUCATION: SOLICITUDE

If we do not shy away from seriously accepting the image of children's angels taking their bodies in hand during sleep, completely enclosing them, imparting to them, with utmost care and exactitude, the formative impulses to which their growth forces must adjust, then we can judge how expectant their mood is as they awaken and confront us. Those children expect strength-ordering reinforcement from us in order that they may feel comfortable in their bodies. They expect our help in establishing a firm body-image such as gives them confidence, based on being formed and enclosed, in their existence. That is the first consideration in developing the touch sense. We must do all we can to assist them in becoming conscious of their skin, so that a distinct imaging of their bodies results. They long to feel themselves enclosed in the gentle firmness of parental hands so that they may perceive themselves in their corporeal individuality and its limitations while simultaneously experiencing that touch need not be the cause of fear but rather of security and closeness. The time comes swiftly when children want to explore their surroundings or activity with touching hands. This requires a certain amount of confidence to keep them from being too frightened by unavoidably painful experiences that accompany such exploration, and, instead, to feel sheltered in their bodily housing, no matter how chilly the wind or wobbly the walls. What began as a bodily-transmitted sense of being enclosed as a positive experience of closeness becomes at a later period one of the building blocks of personality development and world-related egohood. (The opposite would be a feeling of being left without protection, in a state of terror at being touched.) Bodily confidence is the first stage of self-confidence, an elementary experience transmitted by the touch sense, a feeling of dwelling within the borders of one's own body. Whether in later years a person feels psychically and spiritually "at home with himself" and firmly centered, whether he experiences the world of his thoughts and feelings as his own kingdom in which he, rather than the world outside him, is the ruler, depends to a considerable degree on the body-centered, orientating aspect of his early touch sense development. The soul level, however, determines the possibility for other development of that basic security into lively, discriminating interest in the world about, described above as the source of social capacities, such as tenderness, concern for others, participation, and the like.

We foster these developments, if I may repeat myself, by making a child conscious of his skin as his boundary by the confidence-creating way we touch it. I have called it gentle firmness, because the term covers both the boundary-setting aspect of defining and the opening, closeness-generating aspect of gentleness, and it refers to our actual "handling" of the child's body as we care for her and play with her. Let us hope there is a lot of the latter. Shy, hesitant teaching, which may be based on our own fear of contact, has the opposite effect on rendering our handling uncertain and confused and causes similar reactions in the child. An insensitive, unfeeling touch is just as harmful. When we limit ourselves to purely pragmatic hygienic requirements, carrying them out without inner participation, they are experienced as rough, though there may be nothing physically hurtful in them. Lack of participation wounds. What is needed is not some particular technique or other, but rather the acquiring of a certain inner attitude that makes a small but decisive difference in everything we do.

There are obviously concrete measures that can be taken in fostering the touch sense when we observe that a child needs special help in this aspect, but how it is done is what chiefly matters. There is no vast outward difference between bathing your child only because children ought to be clean or because you want to provide him with a sheath that strengthens his confidence in living, but in the experience of children the two procedures are worlds apart.

In cases where there is an obvious touch sense problem, I often prescribe anointing the child's whole body every morning in a certain procedure. But here, too, nothing is gained if this is carried out as a burdensome duty. The child then rejects it instinctively. But if it is done with the right feeling, with a grasp of the deeper significance of this seemingly pointless procedure, if it takes place out of concern for the child's destiny, quite surprising results can come of it. You might hear from teachers that the child's interest and attentiveness have suddenly improved.

For just as restless children need our tolerance, our foresightful true regard, in order to feel more comfortable in their bodies, shy, anxious, and unprotected sensitive children need our deeply participating interest. These are frightened, timid, refuge-seeking children who shy away from everything strange, novel, or unaccustomed. If we want to help them, the most important thing is to observe their touch sense. We must give them the feeling that we have real concern for them and want to be active sharers of their destiny.

I do not mean worried, humorless concern. No child should get the impression that he or she is responsible for the parent's careworn, dejected state. Anxious children always feel guilty for everything. I am speaking rather of an attitude of warm concern that signals to a child that she is safe.

Of course, these children need our tolerance, too; all children do, but especially those who have a hard time relating to themselves and to the world. Where personal esteem is lacking, even the cleverest educational methods are unaffected. For anxious children to have a sense of being solicitously accompanied on their destined path is all important. There is an attitude that should be cultivated in relating to them that I have sometimes encountered in impressionable nurses, of whom it is said that their profession is "bred into blood and bone." Such individuals have an incredibly comforting, encouraging way with them that cures by its mere presence. Energy, decisiveness, understanding, and helpfulness are combined in them to the point where sick people can experience the miracle of feeling their helpless condition to be an actual blessing.

THE LATENT TRAUMA OF THE ANXIOUS CHILD

Anxious children cannot be called sick in the ordinary sense, though we can see that they feel themselves to be so in certain respects. They also perceive themselves as needing care and comforting.

Restless, nervous children do not primarily perceive themselves that way. Their problem is chiefly dissatisfaction with themselves. They feel worthless, and as though they internalize the role of outsiders into which they actually maneuver themselves. This results, sooner or later, in their feeling compelled to confirm everything negative that people think about them: "Look! You see how horrible I am!"

The first thing that needs emphasizing in their case is that genuine regard for them amounts to an absolute elixir of life. This contrasts with the need of anxious, timid children to have attention paid to their easily hurt feelings; the regard we show them has to be of the sort that expresses our concern for them, our fellow feeling. Unlike restless, nervous children, they sense protective closeness and authoritative influencing of their personality core as a strengthening rather than as something to fear. This must not be loveless, intimidating authority, for that only worsens the whole situation. But a goodly proportion of the above-mentioned nursing skill, coupled with parental love makes the best treatment we can give these children, enabling us to reinforce their sheath and form awareness. Anxious children need "gentle firmness." That is true not only with respect to bodily contact but in all phases of everyday intercourse with them.

There is a point, however, where caring topples over into overprotectiveness and becomes burdensome for the recipient. What in the former case provides welcome shelter can be felt by the restless type as imprisonment. That is why the latter so urgently needs us to be magnanimously tolerant, reserved, allowing great freedom of movement, far more freedom than the anxious child usually welcomes. We might say that anxious children tend to feel left in the lurch if they are treated too tolerantly. Our protectiveness is experienced by them as the mark of our caring, whereas restless children take overconcern as a lack of esteem, preferring to be shown that we respect them in spite of everything. The latent trauma of the anxious child being left to his own devices contrasts with the restless child's lack of appreciation.

You can see that it makes good sense to go into these subtle differences and to study children accordingly. I am up in arms against using the term "love of children" to mean a featureless brew. We need to know what we are dealing with in the special context of problems in individual cases. As I stated at the onset, it is perfectly possible to apply genuine insight in ways that bring about gradual changes in attitude and develop a certain skillfulness in a child's handling. Once you have understood that your little "scared rabbit" is suffering from a constant sense of exposure and abandonment—that her latent trauma is that she fears being left in the lurch—your task becomes that of providing the gentle firmness of solicitous protection and security.

Once you have come to see this against the background of a touch sense problem you realize that the child has, for whatever reason, a too indistinct, touch sense-mediated experience of enclosure. All of this effects his angel's comforting and confirming activity into the day, so that the impressions of the senses storming in extinguish all memory of the night. Once all this is not only taken seriously but made the content of your meditative practice every evening—then you will see how you are gradually more and more able to receive the right inspiration at the right moment, to have presence of mind and flexibility in your education. "Fingertip sensitivity" develops. You are reminded of the metaphor of the watcher on the bridge and the challenges he issues before he allows you to question your child's angels. These are, first, to bring with you a clear concept of the child's external aspect and your impression of her behavior patterns, as this results from regular attentive observation, coupled with rejection of all preconceived judgments and evaluations, since not they, but the child, are the point. The second challenge is to have taken real trouble to have your questions clearly thoughtout, without any admixture of self-interest. You have the example of the frightened, fluttering bird as a hint of the way you can proceed to develop imaginative perceptions into practical ideas as you strive for insight.

BODILY AND SOCIAL SENSES: ACQUIRED FEARS

Tolerance, which is a capacity based on developing the life sense, is one of the preconditions for understanding and valuing our fellow humans. To this must be added the touch sense, mediated capacity to establish and enjoy closeness, which comes of a secure sensing of enclosure. That is the soil from which impulses for solicitous concern emerge. We call on a child's initiative readiness to adopt such an attitude, one which he brings from his nightly encounters with his angel, when we exhibit this caring in the child's presence. It is not just our behavior with the child himself that is decisive here, not just the gentle firmness of our care of his body and being in our daily life together, but rather our whole relationship to the world as this finds expression in thousands of small ways and is copied by the child's fine sensing imitativeness. We must be solicitous and careful in our handling of everything about us when we are dealing with scared rabbits. We should develop awareness of the security it gives children to observe considerate treatment of even lifeless objects, for as you know, nothing is ever dead in a young child's conceiving. All rough or careless or loveless handling of objects, plants, animals, and people should be avoided in the presence of an anxious child.

I know that it is asking almost too much when I make such statements, and I am conscious in making them of my own shortcomings in these respects. But much is accomplished by making the effort. Children are wiser than we are; they perceive that we are striving upwards, whereas we grownups are fixated on outcomes.

Tolerance and caring, patience and reverence for the young: these are the virtues for the development of which we need to create favorable conditions by giving sufficient heed to foster the life, and touch-sense complex and keep them in mind in our own conduct.

I use the term "life- and touch-sense complex" for the simple reason that these senses form a unity. From a developmental-psychological standpoint, it is, nevertheless, fruitful, as we have seen, to differentiate, between the areas of the basal sense field affecting the behavioral disturbances or one-sidedness of a child's nature.

It should be noted in passing that the reason why nurturing the basal senses is so important is that they provide the right milieu for the maturing of the higher, insightful social senses. These are: the ego sense, which enables us to have direct experience of the innermost individual core of our fellow human beings, and the thought and speech sense, where we live with understanding into each other's way of thinking and speaking. Lastly, we have the sense of hearing which provides the foundation for all the higher capacities. Here we "listen into" what exists spiritually in the world about us and expresses itself to us as the content of human souls. This is the background, in other words, for the aforementioned functions of the senses of speech, thought, and egohood, which deserve to be called processes of "sublimated hearing."

I just want to suggest here that there really are such senses of understanding as Rudolf Steiner called them, and that they are closely interwoven with the self-perceiving basic functions of the bodily senses insofar as the latter are the nurturing ground in which the higher senses ripen.

The "social senses" are expansive, the means whereby we actively identify with all that is outside us. The bodily senses are contrastingly defensive. They are our means of experiencing ourselves in our relationship with the external world. What may be called the connecting senses of smell, taste, sight, and warmth carry on their "weaving" activity between the opposites.

Now, before we go on to the complex of the senses of motion and balance, let us ask ourselves how it happens that we can be confronted with anxious, timid children in whom the sensing of form and sheathing has not developed properly. What sort of children are these whose particular nature is to not have achieved the sufficiently secure grounding that the touch sense mediates?

Of course every child can have the misfortune of becoming involved in circumstances in which his secure ground collapses or is undermined. There can be traumatic experiences, such as gross neglect, or massive exposure to overstimulation may generate the touch-sense fear syndrome. This can result in the loss of a distinct body image and produce the concomitant psychological trauma described as a feeling of abandonment and unprotectedness, along with fear of contact of every kind and even of manual extension. There can be concern about getting dirty. All these symptoms can appear quite suddenly in children not generally predisposed to such behavior, or they may gradually develop. Young children who are exposed over the years to media habitation, who handle only mechanical or plastic toys and almost never have an experience of loving bodily contact with caring, sheltering adults, can hardly be expected to develop a sense of distinct individual form and enclosure, let alone one of being "permeated with universal cosmic substantiality—with existence as such"—that is a feeling not generated by plastic blocks, electronically steered toy autos, trick films, and Game-Boy computer playthings.

Let us not deceive ourselves: children who do not belong in the fearful, timid category can be driven into it. All that is necessary is to go along with everything presently conceived of as making up the beautiful bright world of childhood while keeping the children themselves at arm's length. That offers the best prospect of generating a fear of life such that by adolescence a tormenting sense of inability to feel one's reality, to feel here at all, makes its appearance. Everything is seen as though through opaque glass.

That is one background to this syndrome. But there is also the distinct type we have come to know here: that of the innately anxious, timid child. And since the establishment of a kind of doctrine is our purpose here, let us look at this obstacle from a type angle.

We have become familiar with the behavioral characteristics of the nervous-aggressive type from the aspect of bodily fear, and saw that though this fear is generated in the very early months and years of life, it is not necessarily the outcome of crude handling on the part of care-giving adults. Children can bring such tendencies with them, and they may be unrecognized as a type until too late, or else the caregivers do not know what to do about it, because no one has given them pertinent information from scientific study. The result is that desirable early consultations have not taken place; things go on undealt with. And commenting on that, I can only say, again and again, that it is never too late to give children the help they need.

The anxious, timid child: observations

I have the feeling that, despite all the seemingly thorough discussion we have been having on the subject of the sense of touch, you may all be sensing incomplete orientation in this area, just as was the case in our study of the life or vital sense. It is certainly the sore point of all typology that the pertinent phenomena very seldom show up in their purest form. There are so many mixtures that sharp outlines cannot be drawn. But it is still possible to define the nature and behavior of children with an injured touch sense in such a way that those of you who have a child of that type will recognize it, even though the description may not apply in every detail.

If you now ask what has made a child that way, I have to say again that just as children have inherent temperaments, so do they have a predisposition to a type, and this predisposition encounters a whole series of influences inherent in the prevailing civilization that strengthen it still further. Our tasks as parents and educators are to provide children with the means of countering these influences. The timid, anxious child's disturbed behavior can thus be viewed in the context of the prevailing world fear, as a particular characteristic of his nature that, under present conditions, can easily go in a pathological direction. It is more exactly described as a phenomenon of lack of bodily confidence, of the basic security which the touch sense conveys. A child has to have this security to enable him to experience himself on the soul plane later as an autonomous, self-contained personality, whose sense of form and boundaries makes it possible to approach the world and other people with interest and participation. That is the basic requirement for development of the caring we have been characterizing.

Now, how does a child that lacks this security behave?

Let us look at a little girl of this type—for it's mostly girls who belong in this category, while boys are most often of the nervous-aggressive type—at the arrival of bedtime.

She puts off the moment as long as possible, scrubbing herself extra slowly and way beyond the demands of cleanliness, talking endlessly all the while. There should obviously be someone there with her, preferably her mother. This evening the child's flood of talk rises higher and higher the closer she feels the moment of saying "good night" approaching, and she starts the usual litany of questioning—whether both parents will be at home that evening, what the plan for tomorrow is, will the door be locked when they go to bed, the lights will be turned out, and will the stove be turned off? Will they be going for a walk? Will they look in on her before they go to bed? What if she cannot sleep, or has a stomachache, or wakes up before they do? May she go to them if she has a stomach ache? If she has to go to the toilet again? Will they leave her door and theirs open a crack? It goes on and on. The questioning has no relevance to getting information as such; it is just an insecure child's need for security, a hope of peaceful sleep once everything is settled.

But the attempt fails. You put the child to bed, tell a story, sing a song, bid her lovingly good night. But that is not the end. You are called repeatedly. The whole reservoir of questions must be asked, more trips to the toilet taken, stolen peeps through the living room door, snatched in passing, just to make sure. Sure of what?

The child herself does not know the answer. Many mothers and fathers try to put on end to the trial by lying down with the little bundle of fear until she falls asleep. That is a well meant deed. But in the long run, it takes a hard toll on the family's peace. I am acquainted with families in which for years on end the parents never spent an evening together, because one of them always laid down with the child and instantly fell asleep. And there was the droll case of a father who complained that he had not seen his wife in a nightgown for several months, only in jeans, even in bed. The man went to a marriage counselor, who later referred the matter to us pediatricians. We found out that the young wife was not wearing her jeans as a chastity belt, but lay down night after night fully dressed beside her daughter, fell asleep there, and got up sometime in the night to totter, drunk with sleep, into the parental bed without undressing. Her husband was naturally frustrated by this; he suspected that the two sleepers had concreted a plot against him. A considerable degree of wedded bliss was restored by instead treating the child's fear of going to sleep.

Fears of that sort, which rise to a peak in the late afternoon and evening, surface frequently in children of the type we are discussing. Caretakers should take note that it is particularly these children who "lose their shape" around four or five P.M. and need a lot of help with their soul boundaries. The second half of the afternoon needs to be given over to very orderly procedures, designed to create feelings of peacefulness and security.

To that end, you will do well to arrange a little "program" before supper, one that the child helps choose, and to carry it out quite regularly every day. The program should consist of two parts, an active one and a listening one.

Modeling is a good choice for the active part. You get the child to form two well-rounded balls of the material to be modeled, one larger and one smaller. A cave can be made of the larger ball, with a little entrance. The smaller one is turned into a mouse, which slips into the cave. Or a nest can be made, with a baby bird in it, or a house for a dwarf; you get the idea.

And now, for the listening part of the program, you tell a fairy tale, or sing, or make some kind of instrumental music. Hold the child very close to you; she wants that bodily contact. Then you wind the program up with five or ten minutes of chatting about this and that.

Now comes the preparing of supper. Nothing could be better than to have the child sitting at the table with you in the kitchen, making a picture or playing some game. You should take care at this time not to go clattering and banging and cursing about your work, but exhibit thoughtfulness and foresight in action, qualities for the child to imitate inwardly and gain security from. Or you can involve the child with you in the preparations, if he or she is of an age to do so.

Anxious children require nourishing but easily-digested suppers. Look up recommendations for a diet formulated to meet stomach and intestinal problems.

PREPARATIONS FOR SLEEP AND FOR STARTING THE DAY

The following are suggestions for helping prepare children of the anxious-timid type for sleep.

First, give the child a warm foot bath with a view to encouraging relaxation. If the rest of the family is gathered in the living room, it is best to go somewhere else. You might bring music making into the picture again. Singing with the child at this time, or playing recorded music, is not recommended, since the object is to emphasize closeness and affectionate care. Foot baths should be administered, but not last more than ten minutes at the longest. Then dry and oil the feet.

Now comes a game called foot-touch guessing. The child closes her eyes and tries with her feet to guess objects placed before her, such as an apple, a lemon, a pinecone, some nuts, an egg, a stuffed animal. For every correct guess a point is awarded, and an agreed upon number of points wins a prize. The game is more fun if both participants try out. The child should concentrate exclusively on the touch experiences, to focus her consciousness wholly into her feet, bringing about the desired effect.

When this has gone on for ten minutes, stop playing, put warmed stockings and heavy shoes on the child, and play the balancing and jumping game. The child puts a copper rod or a book on her head and walks across the room, keeping the object balanced in place. Then she climbs up on something and jumps down hard, three times over, either by herself or holding your hand. Then she repeats the balancing and jumping, three times over, ending with three jumps.

Now the getting to a bed follows, briefly and decisively. Do not allow any long, drawn out, performance, instead direct the procedure with gentle firmness.

If you now envelop the child in a warmed cloth infused with chamomile or yarrow and keep it on during the good-night story, and if you do not forget the evening prayer, you have carried out a creative program of the most effective kind from afternoon to bedtime. This is a prime example of therapeutic education. You will have become your child's therapist and made love a thoroughly practical undertaking. Love must create seeing, not blindness—a seeing fortified for action.

Anxious, timid children are at their best in the morning hours. One evening I asked a child of this type who was to go on vacation to his grandmother's the next day whether he was looking forward to the visit. The child answered, "Well, in the evening everything always seems quite different than it does in the morning. Tomorrow morning I'm quite certain I'll be happy about it." The boy was perfectly familiar with the fear of change that kept growing as evening approached. Such children have the tendency, so different from that of the overactive child, to get stuck in the situations they find themselves in and are fearful of every new adjustment.

Restless, nervous children, quite the contrary, fear having to stay put. It is very helpful, in dealing with both types, for their caretakers to look backward over the day just past and forward to the day to come. But with the restless ones, reviewing (a remaining connected with that has happened) should be emphasized, while with the fearful children, looking ahead (to accept what the future is bringing) is more important. Overactive children should look back over the entire day from its start to its finish, with only a short look ahead. Beginning with the tenth year, the day can also be reviewed in reverse order. Reviewing for the anxious child should be the opposite: very brief, but the day to come should be fully anticipated and prepared for. This look ahead should be repeated as soon as the child awakens the next morning, even before the family sings, welcoming in the day. Five minutes suffice on both occasions.

Please take ceremonies like the evening prayer and the morning singing with all due weight. They must not be brushed aside as unimportant.

Again, the anxious child should receive a full body massage. This is done with the child lying (and kept warm!) and should consist of a massage with some fragrant body care oil. This procedure helps to extend benefits of the sense of form and sheathing which the child's angel has given her in sleep but which tends to pale quickly in the onrushing events of the new day.

EDUCATION AND SELF-ESTEEM: THE POSITIVE OUTLOOK

I am afraid I have been a bit remiss in not keeping to my motto, quoted at the beginning of the book, when I said I was not going to hand out any recipes, but instead discuss some findings made in the anthropological study of the human being that would encourage my listeners to develop ideas of their own. I have gone back to some extent on my resolve. But it may have been some help to you, and it is certainly a pleasure to me, to share a few experiences I have had over the years as I've worked in the fields of child therapy and educational consulting.

But we will not overdo "prescribing." My chief concern is to encourage you to work on your own, to use thorough, exact observation and the kind of meditative practice already recommended, and to acquire the intuitive insight that will guide you in helping your child.

I have brought forth a good deal of material on the sense of touch that illuminates the basic problems encountered by anxious, timid children, and I think that if you read it over not just once, but several times, you will notice that the images provided will begin to work in you. Do not forget, as you study, the main point—observe your child with a lover's attention to detail, take your time rather than hurriedly searching for answers, and always without prior judgments.

What strikes you about your child when you rise above alternating attraction and reaction, expectation and disappointment, and so on? With difficult children, one easily falls into the trap of seeing everything that happens as a confirmation of the fears one has been entertaining. Children, thus negatively prejudged by their disappointed elders, are imprisoned in their displeasing roles; parental behavior actually tends to become an unreceived electing of the very things the child is supposed to stop doing.

The best means of breaking out of this vicious cycle is the above-described practice of unprejudiced observation combined with a refusal to draw conclusions. The important thing is to simply take genuine interest in the child. If you succeed (even if only for ten minutes daily) to the point of cultivating a "positive" prejudgment," you will make gradual progress and extend the practice to the point of saying, "My child has beautiful, endearing, admirable characteristics; I will concentrate quite consciously on these." This is to practice attentive, participatory interest, and you will see how it tends all by itself to work into a loving way of looking at the child.

Opportunity beckons here, and it should be seized upon consciously and used. You will develop an entirely new relationship to your worrisome child if you open yourself to him and make the schooling of your observation a regular exercise.

There is a lot of talk these days about positive thinking. What people generally have in mind is egotistical positive thought about themselves. This is too meager an objective, in my opinion. What is hardly ever mentioned is that other kind of positivity, that positive regard that looks on others with kindliness and empathy. These are not outstanding qualities in modern life, but where they exist they are a deep-down blessing. And a deep-down spirit of the time is urging us to shape our civilization according to the needs of children, to lay hold on the strengths of love and forbearing, these resources from which we can hope for a reorientation of social life on every level.

FURTHER OBSERVATIONS OF ANXIOUS, TIMID CHILDREN

Let us imagine you are parents of an anxious, timid child, always getting angry at the way he acts up at the least excuse. What scenes he makes over having his hair brushed in the morning! But that is not the only aggravation. He moves more slowly the later it gets when it is time to be out of the house en route to school or kindergarten. It seems as though he has had a soporific to drink for breakfast instead of a normal beverage. Yet he was lively enough when he got out of bed. Is he trying to infuriate his mother?

The hands of the clock march relentlessly on. Now the child's shoes pinch. His sweater is scratching. On with other shoes and another sweater! As you are helping him on with his coat, already in a nervous state over the lateness of the hour, you inadvertently scratch his cheek. He emits shrieks as though you had purposely given him a deep, profusely bleeding wound.

That is the way every morning starts. But these problems are mild compared with those of the later hours of the day. What hypersensitivity!

There is an additional facet to the general worsening as the day wears on: clumsiness. The child is continually on the point of falling; she keeps bumping against things; she stumbles over rugs; she plops glasses down so hard that the contents slop out and all over the place.

Now the questioning begins again and picks up speed: "What . . . ? And what . . . ? And what . . . ?" endlessly along with ticks that you have long found irritating: blinking, coughing, nervous swallowing, and the like.

In the afternoon, an increase in these acquired habits intensifies your revulsion. All kinds of perfectly harmless things: substances, noises, or just words (not to mention foods) cause frightful disgust. Concentration diminishes with each passing minute. Doing homework brings on a battle of nerves.

Here we have a further portrait of the anxious, timid type of child. The symptoms I have described speak unmistakenly of the lack of a sense of form and sheathing, of insufficient bodily self-perception, fear of contact. Rudolf Steiner calls this condition one of "soul soreness."

Problems of changing from one situation to another are also part of this syndrome. Individuals who feel secure in their bodies always take a "piece of home" along with them. They never sense themselves being as "away" or unprotected, no matter where they go. But if this basic security is missing, the body has to be "replaced" by one environment that is either already familiar or known to have been proven safe.

So-called "threshold fears," evening and morning aspects of which we have been studying, are generated by the above syndrome. One of them is the fear of parting; for going to sleep means parting, means giving up a sure certainty of return and of the continuance of a familiar world. That certainty substitutes for the security otherwise experienced as a sense of bodily sheathing. Anxious children are afraid that their world could disappear and be gone when they wake up again. They are also hounded by fear of the house burning down and have nightmares about it.

These children are apt to appear like young patricians. They are often handsome, delicately built, light complexioned or even blond, distinguished by their speech facility and rich fantasy. Abstract, logical thinking, and exact reporting come hard to them, although some notice this difficulty and set themselves to overcome it. That is rather rare, however.

Children of this type suffer from breathing problems of bronchial origin sometimes as extreme as spastic bronchitis and asthma, and from cerebral irritations, skin eruptions, and bladder infections. They have a strong liking for ceremonies, solemn occasions, and traditional beauty.

I have often noticed that these children are easily motivated to help others and to make sacrifices for them. They are concerned for others' drawbacks. They long to comfort others in their suffering. But fear often makes them incapable of doing so, and this they find hard to bear.

But you see what an impressive treasure of kindly, sensitive impulses slumbers in them, waiting for a chance to function. We should focus our attention on this fear-fettered potential and help to free it by applying everything we can learn about primary and secondary disturbances of the sense of touch and about what can be accomplished by a consequential pedagogical dealing with them.

This participation in their education is given by angels.

Observe your child, and then try making what you have seen and know into a questioning image that you take with you into sleep. You might try something like the following: "There once lived a princess who always felt naked, no matter how many clothes she put on. Even when she had been given a shield to wear over her chest, a tiny twig, torn off by the wind blew against her, and a wound was found on that spot when she undressed . . . ."

You know that fairy tales have to have happy endings. How would you finish this one?

Overactive and anxious children—these are the two kinds of problem cases of most concern to educators and therapists. Let us make another listing of the key words that indicate direction and should be kept in mind in dealing with pre-elementary school children.

Rhythm
Continuity
Warmth
Carefully considered diet
Bodily well-being
Sleep enhancment
Preserving a relationship to the past
Patience and reverence as educational attitudes
Tolerance as model conduct

We can progress on a straight course, drawing further, uncomplicated conclusions from the above. Isn't the significance of music obvious, and the role water plays on the primal element of well-being? The therapeutic value of practicing leisureliness, of slowing down (for example, where rhythm is concerned) is almost overwhelmingly evident. So is making up stories together to be continued, with consequent action, as preservation of relatedness to the past, as continuity, and so on. Once you have firmly internalized the signal concepts, your life with the child in question will call forth the insight needed for dealing with each concrete situation. That is how professional therapists proceed. Once the general direction is established, the children themselves indicate the right path. We simply need to be attentive and learn to decipher their messages.

I am certainly not saying that you should not seek expert advice. You should, however, communicate your own ideas to therapists who, if they are unburdened by conceit, will rejoice that you already know much of what they would want to tell you. I always welcome cooperation with parents and hope that they will be creative and come up with insightful ideas formed on the basis of mental study of human development. Education is in certain respects a service and a skill as well; fundamental knowledge and practical facility are both required, and both are learnable.

But education is above all an art. Imagine what painters or composers or poets would suffer if they had to have a teacher always there telling them what to do next! Truly artistic acts can be undertaken only in freedom, with all the joy and despair that goes with them. And that holds true of education.

What are the key words in the education of anxious, timid children? I will list them:

Nearness
Protection
Skin care
Comfortable natural clothing
Development of touch experience
Concern for the quality of touch objects
Giving protective shape to evening hours
Preparatory training for the following day
Gentle firmness as educational attitude
Solicitude as model conduct

Isn't it perfectly obvious that playing with earth and stones, as well as modeling and sculpturing, should be recommended? Caring for plants and making a garden should be made available. Suitable therapeutic fairy tales should be sought out, and children should be encouraged to make up stories of their own.

I will leave it at that, but remind you that the points to keep always in mind are:

Rejection is the restless child's basic trauma. Being left to his/her own devices is the anxious child's basic trauma.

These two types are, as stated, the ones of most concern. That is why I have made them the focus of our deliberations and devoted correspondingly ample space to discussions of the life and touch senses. The special angle chosen for that purpose has been to ask what social-economical qualities children's angels want to implant in the receptacles that healthily developed bodily senses offer. What soul harvest is the soil being cultivated for in each case? What aspect of children's imitative readiness to support the good is strengthened in each case by parting these senses?

The theme that runs through our deliberations here like a subterranean stream that keeps breaking through to the surface is moral education, but moral education from an entirely different viewpoint than what we usually encounter. This enables us to arrive at a common understanding: that tolerance is the eventual fruit of the life sense, strengthened by ordering, harmonizing support from the spiritual world. Caring as a life-long characteristic is the fruit of spiritually supported, forming and nurturing of the sense of touch. We do our part when we keep in mind the educative measures listed above. In the surrounding world, perception conveyed by the sense of touch is an ongoing, changing experience. It plays a subordinate role in the active intercourse between the ego and the world as a means of "investigating the unknown," as Shenrle puts it. Its primary function is in perceiving the particular overall state of being or disposition of an individual's structural complex as it gradually finds its way into the incarnation and settles down in later years.

There will, however, always be statistics that threaten the basic security thus established. The measure we take to develop and support young children's touch sense will help their incarnation process and build resistance to later challenges to their basic security.

The same holds true for the other basic senses. The important thing is always to keep in mind the particular nuances of the incarnation process and, with appropriate educational support, to guarantee lifelong security.

4.

A Study of the Senses of Motion and Balance

INTRODUCTION

The circle of the four body-centered, self-perceptive senses is closed by turning to the senses of motion and balance. We ask ourselves what the later soul capacities are that we prepare the ground for by devoting our educational attention and support to those two areas of the incarnation process?

The term "incarnating process" is understood to mean the various aspects of the uniting of the soul and spirit with the bodily physical elements. An important factor in this accomplishment consists in a child's acquiring a definitive capacity to perceive his own bodily states as related to his surroundings. Precisely expressed, the perceptions in question are those that reflect the way the soul relates to the body and its processes. I am speaking about those in which the dynamics are always partly determined by the nature of that relationship. We were able to see this clearly in the case of the touch senses where the skin serves both in establishing a border and in being a mediating zone with the world. One function is protective, and the other is sensitive. The former supplies the forming, sheathing element, while the latter provides what I have called the "resonance" and allows us to gain a sense for ourselves in everything we encounter.

We can see clearly that we are dealing here with a perception of our own overall body-soul state in its (involuntary) intercourse with the surrounding world, a perception conveyed by the sense of touch in ongoing, changing experience. Only in second or third place does this sense also play a role in the active intercourse between the ego and the world as our means of "investigating the unknown," as Shenrle puts it, and in determining distance and familiarity. It is primary function is in perceiving the particular overall state of being or disposition of an individual body and soul as they move through their life's journey.

There will, however, always be situations that threaten the basic security thus established. The measure we take to develop and support young children's touch sense will help their incarnation process and build resistance to later challenges to their basic security.

The same holds true for the other basal senses. The important thing is always to keep in mind the particular nuances of the incarnation process and, with appropriate educational support, to guarantee lifelong security.

EXPERIENCING ONESELF AS A FREE SOUL

Rudolf Steiner characterized the sense of motion as that whereby we experience our own movement, from blinking to moving our legs. It registers unconsciously in everything that goes on in our system of limbs and muscles when we move. Karl König writes in his book, *The Child's First Three Years*, that "every muscle-movement requires the cooperation of the entire system of voluntary muscles. That also holds true of the speech musculature; it participates fully in the activity of the total motor system." When we walk or dance or just bend a little finger, the whole active or passive musculature has to be involved in the intended course of action.

These movements are masterly acts of coordination and compositional skill continuously carried out by our subconscious, and we perceive ourselves involved in them through the sense we have of our own motion. We can speak here of an instinctive perceptive capacity, of an extremely subtle "tracking" that goes on under the threshold of consciousness. But what takes place at that unconscious level enables us to make use of our physical bodies as tools of motion such that they respond with the most delicate sensitivity to our motive impulses or accompany external movement with "understanding." This has an effect on our overall sensing of aliveness.

Rudolf Steiner called this activity ("radiated upward into our soul life by the sense of movement"), an experiencing of oneself as a "free soul." The sense of touch mediates our awareness of form and of an ongoing connectedness with the divine, the life sense, our awareness of well-being, and the sense of motion, the feeling of being free. We now have what might be called "shelter in God's hands" and, in addition to the well-being of resting in oneself, a sensing of freedom, more exactly expressed as "bodily experienced free soul mobility," Rudolf Steiner said of this, "The sense of motion, of what is going on in us as, in the shortening or lengthening of our muscles, we perceive whether we are walking or standing, jumping or dancing, whether and how we are moving, rays into our souls that feeling of freedom that allows us to sense ourselves as souls. That you feel yourselves to be free souls is due to the outward radiating of the sense of motion."

Please do not forget that what we are speaking of here is of feelings that do not usually come to full consciousness. They do so only when we become aware that we don't have them. A person who is suffering from frightful terror, for example, perceives very painfully that he has lost the basic security supplied by the touch sense; his awareness of form and sheathing, of "finding shelter in God's hands," disappears, and everything seems unreal to him. Individuals tormented by restlessness, nervousness, poor concentration, and forgetfulness surely notice that the basic awareness of well-being, relaxation, and continuity supplied by the life sense that they used to take for granted is no longer there; that comfortable sensing of themselves as space-filling selves in bodies. As long as everything is in order, we do not notice the ongoing subconscious perceptions and related basic body-soul experiences that form the foundation of our sensory existence and without which we would not be equal to living.

Now let us examine the effects of a lack of the basic security provided by the sense of motion, looking first at its positive aspects. The fact that we sense ourselves rooted, as soul-endowed beings, in the stability and reliability of our bodily existence (the life sense) and "maintained in form" by our physical shape—or, we may say, by form-creating and form-preserving forces (the sense of touch)—while nevertheless able to develop free inner mobility within its framework, explains why we perceive ourselves to be autonomous on the soul level. Here the physical body, rather than presenting an obstacle, acts as a sensitive, pliant instrument, providing us with "a dreamlike sureness."

The word "autonomous" is usually used to denote works presented under the maker's name. In logic, autonomy means a proper name. In both cases it suggests "ego." Thus, we can speak of autonomy on the soul level in reference to a feeling of freedom, of self-determination in shaping our lives.

The life sense must be thanked for experience of biographical continuity. We have to thank the sense of touch for our capacity to experience that continuity pictorially as a structural entity evolving an interchange with the world. But it is the sense of motion that enables us to be aware that we owe our experiencing of autonomy to it. According to Rudolf Steiner, the sensing of autonomy is based on a "raying into our souls" in *stati nascendi* "of experiences of the unconsciously functioning sense of motion." That is the primal phenomenon here. We have to "notice" ourselves making motions in order to move freely. Conversely, we would not be able to notice them properly if we were constantly losing control of ourselves; we would be extremely irritated as we perceived our own movements.

Now imagine something happening to make us lose control so that we would begin gesticulating wildly and floundering around. Maybe we sat down in an anthill and had to spring up, doing what could almost qualify for St. Vitus dance. Or let us say some wasps flew at us, making us beat the air and shake our heads, hitting ourselves on the nose.

Could we say that we had a sure sensing of the sequence of our motions in cases like these? Hardly! Instead of being able to ascertain a "sense of ourselves as free souls," we felt completely beside ourselves. The certainty surely transmitted by the sense of motion is the product of a really well-orientated awareness of sequential movement. The fact that it remains unconscious does not mean that it is unreliable. Quite the contrary, unconscious orientation is the most reliable kind there is, provided nothing interferes with it.

The best orientation through the sense of motion comes from a "fine tuning" of our unconscious perception of purposeful sequences of movement. That gives us certainty in motion. It also gives us certainty with respect to an inner accompanying of movement outside us. Schenurle explains that "we ourselves have to move inwardly if we are to perceive movement." For it is not external motion that the sense of motion perceives, but rather the inward motion that accompanies it. We perceive ourselves in our inward accompanying of the motion outside us.

What I am talking abut here is not perception of objects, but of movement. When we follow the flight of a bird, our sense of sight helps us perceive the bird itself in the various positions of its flight path, but it is due to the sense of motion that accompanies sight that we are able to "understand" that the bird is moving from one place to another at a certain speed. If we lacked the sense of motion, we would have no means of grasping that the bird's changing bodily postures and its changing spatial placement have a meaningful connection that results in its flight path. We could "understand" neither the fact that the bird is flying, nor the how of it, if we were not to accompany it inwardly and to experience ourselves doing so. Thus, we are justified in saying that every perception we have of movement is either directly or indirectly the perception of our own motion. In a general discussion of the basal senses Rudolf Steiner said, "The interesting fact is, though what we perceive is definitely a subjective inner perception, the processes involved are, nevertheless, wholly objective." He says elsewhere that though such motion as bird flight or the swaying of treetops in the wind is objective, our inner perception of them is decidedly subjective.

Motion of a chaotic, hectic, disconnected nature that is suddenly broken off or ill-suited to the time span in which it is taking place has a similar effect on the sense of motion, both when we ourselves are the perpetrators or are exposed to it—such as the effect loud bangs or shrill, unpleasant noises have on our sense of hearing. Such experiences strain the senses.

The sense of motion is in its element wherever movement makes sense. When our overall body-soul condition is such that in its involuntary intercourse with the world we feel ourselves to be free and mobile beings, integrated into that world's movement patterns, when we have a simultaneous experience of both sovereignty and connectedness, this results in a definite soul grounding.

This groundedness is not ordinarily noticed. It makes itself felt below the conscious level as a continuously upward raying—or perhaps just a weak shimmering—a brightness that can never be wholly darkened by the various needs, miseries, and fears that we may have to contend with.

I would like to call this grounding, "freedom-based world connectedness." It is what gives us, even in seemingly hopeless situations, the confidence to summon up a new impulse to move on in life, to change direction, to develop initiative. If someone has really suffered a hard defeat but can adapt an attitude of, "So be it for now, on to the next!", meaning it rather than just saying it, then his grounding with respect to his sense of his own motion is in very good shape; he has a well-developed feeling of autonomy. His "So be it!" expresses a conclusion about the past comeuppance. "What's the point of staring at what's happened as something bad that can no longer be changed? Now it's just become part of my biography that must be accepted." Whereas his, "On to the next!" expresses his confidence in his ability to act, his sensing of himself as a free soul looking ahead. Autonomy, a feeling transmitted by the sense of motion, differs from the well-being transmitted by the life sense and the awareness of form and sheathing transmitted by the sense of touch in that it possesses a marked kinship with the future.

There is still another aspect to consider—the perception of oneself free in one's own mobility. This has been characterized as the basic stage and primal phenomenon of a developed sense of motion and has thus far been examined solely from the standpoint of an individual's own bodily movement and the movement carried out as an accompaniment to the physical movement of objects in the surrounding world.

We have noted that the ability to sense and perceive undergoes a metamorphic process in the case of both the life and touch senses, and the same holds true of the sense of motion.

So we must ask what the abilities are that the sense of motion produces on the purely psychological level; what sublimations does it give rise to?

The genius of language indicates the direction in which to seek the answer. When we have some gripping experience, we speak of it as "moving."

What is it that is moved in such a case? It is the inner human being. On a higher level, the sensing of that inner motion is a self-perceptive process in which we observe our feeling life and the movement taking place there as the result of interchange with the outer world and with our fellow human beings.

Our ability to perceive our own inner stirrings also enables us to understand and participate in the soul stirrings of others. I will just remark in passing that accompanying somatic motion, too, is involved here to the extent that our vegetative processes are stirred by our feelings. But what chiefly interests us is the phenomenon of free mobility on the purely soul level. The sensing of autonomy contemplated on that level derives from the fact that we are not determined by reflected, passing, abruptly changing, unstable, unrelated states of feeling due to a particular situation, but rather self-experiencing occupants of our feeling world and as such in a position to provide for stability and connectedness.

Chaotic, hectic, and discontinuous states also occur, of course, in human soul life. They are processes just as irritating on the soul level to a sensing of our own movement as uncontrolled movement is on the somatic level, and this results in wiping out any feeling of being a free soul. We experience that feeling to the extent that we are able to orientate ourselves in our life of feeling, both in relation to ourselves and to our environment in fluid transition. The latter case should be especially emphasized.

Anyone with the least understanding of the human psyche knows how much freedom suffers from blindness to the feelings of our fellow humankind. "Freedom-disposed relating to the world" rests, as we have seen, on synchronizing sovereignty (independence, self-determination) and connectedness. That holds true in particular in commercial situations. It is sometimes asserted in psychology courses that we are not in conscious control of our feeling life– it is far more easy to be thinking. That is certainly the case. Though we are apt to deceive ourselves about our ability to control our thinking, we are to some extent able to discipline it, as, for example, in carrying out a logical exercise with the fewest possible associative distractions. Control of this kind is totally alien to the life of feeling. It would prove fatal to a capacity that is by nature so intolerant of being forced into rigid form.

We, therefore, had something quite different in mind in speaking above of independence and self-determination; not the steering carried out in thought processes, but "fine-tuning." And how is this conceived?

Our musculature is the model for it. This may sound strange at first. But just consider how every single movement we make requires an accompanying motion throughout the system of our voluntary muscles. This means that we are always moving as a totality. It is never just a part of us moving. Our whole muscular and limb system moves with every motion in a delicate nuance, linking tension and release, shortening and stretching. We know instinctively what muscle sections must accompany the movement we make in stretching out an arm, for example.

And that is not all. Every impulse to motion instantly calls forth a complementary motive impulse—the stretching of an arm evokes an energy current (referred to by Rudolf Steiner as "an astral streaming") which tends to revoke, or to reabsorb, the movement. This prevents the outgoing motion from overshooting the mark. As Rudolf Steiner puts it, "Whenever a change of physical position occurs in our organism, an astral current moves in the opposite direction. This happens when we blink an eye or move our legs. This inwardly experienced balancing process is a product of the activity of our sense of our own motion."

Here we have the prototype: total muscular involvement and complementary equalizing impulses.

A similar balancing process takes place in inner movement and excitation. We participate as whole human beings in every stirring of our feelings. We perceive every finest emotional change and react instinctively to avoid being inwardly divided, pulled out of balance by our sympathies or overwhelmed by grief. Our feeling life is like a moving picture in its relationship to its surroundings, an ever-changing composition of form and color in which red or blue, roundness or angularity, a plane surface or linearity predominates, according to the situation. In every case an invisible artist is at work with a fine sense for the pictorial process and concerned with keeping the composition whole and complete.

We are the invisible artists, and that fine sense is the inner perceiving of our own motion. We will see that, here again, complementary equalizing impulses play a very decisive role.

FINE-TUNING THE SOUL

We can say, slightly modifying Rudolf Steiner's statement, that "whenever a change occurs in our feeling, an opposite complementary astral motive-impulse is set going, and there is revealed in this inwardly experienced process the sublimated activity of the sense of our own motion." If you parents were to be delighted or annoyed about something and the complementary soul coloring were not immediately to put in an instructive polar opposite appearance—a scarcely noticeable elegiac mood countering your delight, say, or a slight wafting of satisfaction countering your annoyance—or if you did not set an opposite stirring in motion at every experience of a strong feeling, you would be delivered over, helpless, to your moods. And we often are, as everybody knows; we may suddenly be seized by a surge of emotion powerful enough to overwhelm any sensing of our own motion; and the invisible artist cannot react with the necessary speed. The popular term for this is "blind rage," though it is not the eyes that are blind, but rather self-perception by the soul.

In such cases people say they cannot remember what they did. Legally, this is called impairment of the capacity to judge.

It is not just anger that precipitates this sort of blindness; joy, grief, fear, pleasure, disgust, and so on, can reach a point that blinds us. Fine-tuning of the soul ceases, compositional sensing is obliterated, complementary equalizing becomes ineffective. When this happens to us as adults, we feel, looking back, that we were ill. And that is correct, for a sudden loss of one's external or internal orientation is pathological.

Now, please do not think that I am pleading for a false ideal of poise of the kind so admired by people who look upon strong feelings as indecorous. They are suffering from a guilt complex that may afflict all of us to some degree, but in their case it is excessive. The fact is that such fanatics are driven by a fear that they might be punished for some special happiness by an equally profound unhappiness. So they are never really happy. That is a pitiable condition, and it is due to complete misunderstanding of the principle of harmonizing balance. There is probably no one who has not had to wrestle, on some occasion or other, with this odd guilt feeling anchored deep in the collective subconscious. And up to a certain point it makes sense, in that it guards us against vanity and hedonism. Is it not true, for example, that it seems a "sin" for an individual to disclaim any responsibility for the state of entanglement in guilt that the whole human race has been involved in creating? But people who get on the wrong track in such matters can never be merry. If they let their fear of joy and pleasure and high spirits affect their relationship with the rest of the world and want to dictate to it, a great deal of harm is done to communal life. So I am not pleading for anything, and least of all for any complex-laden enmity to feeling that threatens colorfulness and, for fear of shadows cast by light, wants to contain the sun. What is needed is the invisible artist who is at home with color and can relate light and shadow, preserving the soul's wholeness.

We would not be able to dance without this inner composition whose business it is to fine-tune our mobile organisms. And that goes for the feeling level, too.

Anyone who works with children knows that their "inner composure" is still in the learning stage. This exposes them to constant immersion in the most intense moods that change without any logical transition from one situation to the next and are chiefly due to external causation. The parents' job here is to keep those moods within bounds and to balance them. Depressed children must be comforted, the overexcited calmed, the timid heartened.

We grown-ups usually do this comforting and calming and heartening work on ourselves, for we possess a fine sense of our own inner movement and are, therefore, instinctively able to detect threatening stumbles and losses of balance in the making, and we try to avoid them. This instinct is due to the fact that we experience ourselves as relatively free in our feeling life and have a sense of being free souls.

This experience of independence comes into existence at its basic level as a result of our being "plugged-in to" an unconscious but sensitive fine-tuning of our own sequences of bodily movement, and it is deepened by experiencing ourselves as "composers" in the sphere of our feelings, though this, too, is largely unconscious.

However, these unconscious processes have a noticeable effect on our overall general soul state. How does it happen that we are not continually torn between changing moods and "stay in one piece," despite all the fluctuations and our mobility and our susceptibility to influences? Our soul life demonstrates basic dependability, independence, and connectedness.

Young children do not yet possess this basic sense. They have not, as yet, an ongoing perception of themselves as patterned souls, whose patterning is a continually ongoing mobile process, a structure of motion which, though it constantly changes in interchange with the surrounding world, remains reliable and connected, something that has grown into a mobile form in the course of its biographical development. Small children obviously are not ready for this experience. They do not feel themselves to be "freely mobile beings, meaningfully integrated into the world's movement patterns." The synchronicity of independence and connectedness mediated by the sense of motion needs time to establish itself as a component of basic sensory experience.

DEVELOPING THE CAPACITY FOR EMPATHY AND COMPASSION

The life sense-transmitted feeling of well-being that re-appears on the soul level as a capacity for patience and rever-ence lays the foundation for the social virtue of tolerance. The touch-sense-mediated sensing of form and boundaries is needed for the development of participatory awareness which enables us to develop true caring for others. Neither of these two is ca-pable, as yet, of establishing the feeling of freedom based on the sense of motion whereby we are enabled to shape our relation-ship with our surroundings and our fellow humans so that we become flexible and adaptable without danger of losing our-selves. Liveliness and grace in social situations, the ability to communicate and converse, are not gifts that some individuals are born with and others lack; the first and basic prerequisite for acquiring them is the orientational security provided by the sense of motion. The moral quality thus engendered and described above follows as a matter of course on that basic development. Theoretically speaking, what would be the good of any amount of tolerance and participatory attentiveness if we could not share others' moving expectations?

The question is purely theoretical, for as a matter of fact, that movement-begotten quality is included not only in what has been said about the touch sense, but about the life sense as well. In describing any basal field of perception, a description of all the other fields is implied.

Take the elements, for example. We could not make any statements about water as it occurs in nature if we eliminated any statement about air and heat and gravity. Yet, these are clearly four different qualities that affect our existence in quite different ways. The same holds true of the basal senses.

And so, to repeat, what good would tolerance and par-ticipatory attentiveness do us if we could not share the experi-ences that move others? For all our tolerance, we would remain unparticipating onlookers, totally without understanding. Only the capacities supplied by the sense of motion enable us to participate lovingly to form inwardly moving relationships.

The previous gift of empathy, which might also be called a capacity to sympathize, can be traced here to its background and seen in its developmental history. Sensibility to the inner uniqueness and subtler soul structure as well as to the needs and vulnerability of our fellow men, characterized above as a higher sense of touch, is enhanced thereby, and only through that enhancement does it make its presence known.

For those familiar with sense theory it might be added, to avoid misunderstanding, that the ego sense, which is very closely correlated with the sense of touch, penetrates a still deeper level of others' uniqueness and soul structure. Perceptions of another's being for which descriptive terms exist are sublimated touch sensations, whereas the unique individuality perceived by the ego sense cannot be described in words.

WRONG CONCLUSIONS; DEVELOPMENTAL BLOCKS

We now confront a very remarkable fact of human soul life: in order to feel our way into others' beings, to participate in the movement of their inner experiencing, we require the ability to "sense oneself as a free soul." Individuals who do not possess this capacity at its basic level are incapable of developing true sympathy. Altruism and freedom are indivisibly linked.

Remarks of this kind are scarcely suited to the times. But that does not make them any less true. It is a fact that we have to have achieved the basic security transmitted by the sense of motion to be really able to feel with our fellow human beings. Our compassionate capacity is founded on the freedom with which we relate to the world.

This is certainly not meant as an assertion that a person whose mobility has not developed properly cannot feel sympathy. A dogmatic statement of that kind would be absolutely abhorrent. Although there is an undeniable connection between motion and speech development, there are partially lame children who learn to speak, obviously having acquired the ability to walk upright purely inwardly as a matter of pure inner imitation, in preparation for learning their mother tongue. And there are actually children whose paralysis is such that they cannot make use of their speech organs, but nevertheless learn their mother-tongue purely inwardly. In recent months, newspapers carried the story of a severely autistic young man, Binger Sellin, who, though not paralyzed, had never spoken. Everyone thought he was extremely retarded. One day, with his mother's help, he began communicating by means of a computer. It then became apparent that he was a greatly gifted poet.

I hate to think how many children and young people are being treated in curative homes and psychiatric institutions for retardation when the fact is that they are highly developed souls in unusable bodies. It would be equally mistaken to say that if a child's mobility is injured, it cannot experience itself as a free soul nor, later on, develop compassion. Developmental psychology needs to guard against drawing such conclusions. The fact that a positive connection exists between free bodily mobility, a sensing of inner freedom, and a capacity to feel compassion, does not justify stating the reverse. But if difficulties exist at the basic level, we are justified in speaking of expected problems of development.

It is also true that abilities developed under difficult circumstances often come to especially impressive blossoming, though we should not let this influence us in the direction of a comforting relativism that says, "Well, we all have our destiny." That would be to neglect our responsibility as educators. It is our job to create maximally advantageous conditions for children's favorable development and to do everything we possibly can to ease their problems.

This simply implies recognizing problems of a child's individual destiny and readying ourselves to give help where it is needed. In the case of children with mobility problems, for example, we should not think that their sense of motion can be disregarded. Just the opposite, they need the basic security transmitted by that sense exactly as much as other children do. But the basic level of free bodily mobility has either to be skipped or partially sacrificed, with emphasis in their case on purely inner imitative experience of human and environmental motion. Helping them with this is an important curative-educational task that may have decisive consequences for their whole lives.

Laymen, and even shortsighted so-called experts, shake their heads at the strangeness of seeing curative eurythmists in anthroposophical curative homes dancing around in front of children in wheelchairs. Dancing around is, of course, not what they are doing. They are making use of a carefully studied gestural language to call upon such children's imitative powers, including the sense of motion.

It would be a great mistake to omit from the schoolwork of children with problems of bodily mobility these movement-based parts of the curriculum that play such an important role in Waldorf schools. Instead, special emphasis should be placed on providing extra amounts of opportunity for playful movement in shaping the curriculum so that these children can join in, wherever possible, and otherwise look on. Even if they cannot do the movements, they participate in them inwardly, and that is the important thing. Their inner imitative powers need to be strengthened; that is basic for children with mobility problems. They need help to avoid being made lonely by their limitations, or, worse still, made timid. These are the worst dangers threatening spastic children whose condition keeps them from imitating properly. They find it hard to fit flexibly into social situations. If these grow hectic, the challenge is too great, because such children are not adept at the speedy reactions necessary for dealing with, say, sudden situation changes and, therefore, suffer continuously from feelings of inadequacy. I have had the experience of seeing children so profoundly affected that they get cramps whenever there is overexcited movement in their vicinity.

Granted, such cases are extreme. But they serve impressively to illustrate the important function of the sense of motion.

DEPRESSED, BROODING CHILDREN;
CHARACTERISTICS OF LATENT DISTURBANCES OF THE SENSE OF MOTION

The sense of motion is that which makes us inwardly adaptable to what is going on in our environment. When we are exposed to impressions of movement, we "neutralize" them, so to speak; by accompanying them with our own inner imitative motioning, we are equal to them to the extent that we experience that imitative process, and we react accordingly. In adults this is a purely inner activity. What begins in young children as overt imitation turns increasingly inward, eventually becoming the unconscious perception content of our sense of our own movement.

When the boundary of our orientational capacity is reached here, we are quite definitely aware of the fact. Feelings of helplessness surface. We literally lose our perspective, become timid and clumsy, and feel as though we did not belong in the picture. We stand there at a loss in the midst of goings-on that are not without effect on us. If our impressions are very intense, panic ensues. We want to flee, but instead find ourselves flapping aimlessly around. At such times, the security transmitted by the life and touch senses also breaks down, since, as has been shown, all these senses work together.

But it is not only in especially tumultuous situations that we can lose our inner adaptability and movement-accompanying capacity; it can occur in the midst of some perfectly ordinary conversation. We suddenly notice that we are not "with it"; the thread is lost. We hear the other people speaking and have a fairly good intellectual grasp of what they are saying, but we are somehow not part of it. This makes us feel lonely and timid. If some participant of the group addresses us, we become startled. Does this sound familiar?

Now some expert in the field of sense theory could participate and say that this is a problem of the "higher" senses, of the language and conceptual and ego senses. I would not disagree. But there are relationships of a symbiotic nature between the senses, and in the case of the basal senses there is an indissoluble relationship with the so-called "understanding" senses. That is a theme that cannot be more fully explored here. What concerns us with regard to the basal senses in the example of losing ourselves in a conversation is, along with much else, chiefly the irritation of the sense of motion. It is quite legitimate in this connection to term this sense "the sense of accompanying motion" in order to emphasize that special aspect of its metamorphosed activity, the aspect in which it engages in social processes of accompanying motion.

It helps to try to recall such occasions when we suddenly get a feeling of being as though paralyzed and unable to go on participating in a conversation or social gathering. One's reaction is less that of panic and purposeless action than it is of timidity and exclusion, and one feels frightened, like a young bird that has fallen out of the nest.

Wouldn't we call this essentially a depressed state of mind? The usual reason for it is an inability to free oneself of certain problems one has that forcibly obtrude themselves on one's thinking and feelings, largely due to an obsessive preoccupation with oneself.

It is a good idea to analyze ourselves in moments like these, when we tend to be unable to participate rightly in what is going on around us. We learn in this way to understand children as well as ourselves, as sufferers from a disturbance of the sense of motion, prone to alarm, timidity, and loneliness.

Now, let us turn from focusing on children with obvious mobility problems who can be so greatly helped by the described intensive stimulation of their inner imitative powers and by being maximally included in group games involving motion, gestures, and dialogue with an emphasis on interaction. Let us go on to contemplate children who seem externally to have developed normally, but who cause us concern because, from the age of three or four on, they exhibit a decided and increasing tendency to brood and be self-absorbed, to feel lonely and almost pathologically antisocial and shy of contact. This comes from their withdrawing in timid alarm the moment conflict threatens in their play with other children.

In kindergarten, these children tend to sit alone, playing, perhaps, with blocks, but not really absorbed in what they are doing. That goes on more or less mechanically as they look far away, moving their lips in whispered conversation with themselves. When circle games are played, they stand there forlornly or run in wrong directions. Their bodily posture makes one think of the sad knight in the story book. If they are addressed in a firm voice, they jump as though startled by a loud gunshot.

That is a brief description of the type of child whose sense of motion is not in order and whose "sensation of being a free soul" has not developed properly. What is lacking here is that free relationship to the world that, in children, is an accompaniment of joy in motion. (And I do not mean the wild, boisterous euphoria in moving that is not only good but actual necessary for children with the temperament for it, but rather the quiet enjoyment of purposeful movement that is really pleasure in imitating.)

All pleasure in movement has its origin in early childhood's imitative responses, and all joy in life comes from pleasure in moving—internalized pleasure in moving. A child's uninhibited imitation familiarizes it with the world of motion, of human movement. He imitates first other's upright stance and then their walking. He learns his mother-tongue and to interpret and imitate others' body language, expressed in gesture and habitual motion. Later on, he delights in finger games and circle play, in pantomime and dancing, and, most of all, in copying what his parents and other people do in ordinary living. His unquenchable thirst for movement leads on to a desire to experience freedom in feeling akin to the wind and to birds, and from imitating them to climbing, hopping, racing, roller-skating, biking, performing circus feats, and all sorts of sports.

Children's normal preference is to do these things, whenever possible, in couples or groups, for pleasure in moving and in group dynamics are two sides of the same thing.

There are, of course, children who tend temperamentally and constitutionally to be lazy and slow moving. We should not let this worry us unless they display the above-described symptoms of disturbances of the sense of motion or of weak imitative powers.

BACKGROUND: IMITATIVE WEAKNESS IN EARLY CHILDHOOD

Children who brood or are easily alarmed, who tend to be timid and nonjoiners, lack adequate imitative capacities. We must look in that direction for the root of this weakness. Children of this kind, whose troubles can be attributed to any number of causes (and not necessarily to mistakes made in educating them) have not sufficiently developed a sense of their own movement. They, therefore, lack the basic security, referred and described to here as a "free relationship to the world," transmitted by the sense of motion. Imitative activity has sufficed for them to learn, like other children, to stand upright and to walk and speak. But they have not advanced to the point of feeling suffused from head to toe with the energy to move, to engage themselves in activities around them with their own playful, gestural, and dancing activity in the subtle music of social intercourse. Something has been left halfway to the goal in the development of their sense of motion. This leaves them without the sensation of having the "inner compositor" about which we have talked, with the result that they are not able to make the emotional adjustment called here the fine tuning of the soul. They do not feel as though they belong, but instead always are dropouts in social situations; they cannot grasp what is really going on.

This is not to be blamed on low intelligence, though this type of child often finds it hard "to get the idea." It is rather due to weak development of the sense of motion, and this in turn to a reduction, from whatever cause, of imitative activity in early childhood. Children can be born this way; that is no different in the case of the basal (or bodily) senses than in the sense of sight, either with or without the involvement of problems of heredity.

There are acquired weaknesses, too. In the case of imitation, children can be harmed by too many and too powerful sense impressions which they cannot digest. Media influences of every kind belong in this category, as does too little guarding against optical and acoustical imitation in general, and constant changing of place in car and air travel. Opposite situations also have their dangers in sensory deprivation, as in cases where a child is left alone a great deal. A child's imitative capacity is suppressed when it is subjected to impressions of hot-tempered people, not to mention physical abuse. It is important to see that he or she gets enough sound sleep.

As a matter of principle, good situations are those peaceful, comprehensible ones in which children can spend time quietly observing.

These are the most vital points. But even if parents have nothing to reproach themselves with on these scores, their child can still suffer from a latent weakness of the sense of motion. Sometimes, to come right out and say it, nothing remains to us but to look on the problem as obviously karmic and not due to any other of the usual single causes.

The angel's touch: children's unconscious longings

It is possible for parents to work from the *night side* too, building their children's ordering and harmonizing activity, whereby the life sense is enabled to develop. This will give the children a deep unconscious experience of tolerance raised to the level of love's caring, causing them to turn with longing expectation to seek the same quality in their other human companions. We satisfy this longing when, with calm, reverential attention, we do everything possible to make them feel at home in their bodies and to let them sense in us "that tolerance, raised to the level of love's caring," which characterizes true tolerance in human social life.

Restless, nervous children have a special need of reassurance that we are aiding and abetting their angels' activity in this respect, for they find it difficult to make proper use of the ordering and harmonizing forces flowing to them from their sleep. They resemble people who, having learned something that requires concentration and collectedness for its practice, cannot apply it because they get overexcited. We can picture this happening to every nervous, restless child every time she parts from her angel and confronts life's ordinary problems.

Additionally, we can go on building on the forming-configuring support of the angels whereby the sense of touch can be developed. As a result of this support, children have a deep unconscious experience of that "quality of structuring authority, raised to the level of loving caring." They turn to us with the longing expectation of finding in us that same ordering involvement. We satisfy their longing if we strengthen their sensing of form and boundaries on both a bodily and soul level, doing so with genuine educational enthusiasm (otherwise it is no use), and assuring them of the constancy, the protectiveness, the sure guidance of our caring.

Anxious, timid children have special need of protection. More than other children, they feel deserted when they part from their guardian angels and feel helplessly abandoned to life's dangers. It is our job to substitute for the angel in such cases, and that is chiefly a matter of attitude. Anxious children need people around them who give them the feeling that they will never be left unsupported. This applies to thoughts and feelings as well.

This is a need of restless children also, though they need even more to feel sure of our respect, "no matter what." For their basic trauma is to be unwanted, whereas anxious, timid children are more afraid of being left to their own devices.

RELATING TO DEPRESSED, BROODING CHILDREN

We have already discussed the basic trauma of the depressed, brooding child and shown that it is a fear of being socially left out. He has a feeling of unrelatedness, of not belonging, of not understanding situations.

The important thing is, therefore, to involve such "shut-out" children maximally in everything we do, explaining matters to them in ways suited to their age, getting them to notice connections between things they are experiencing and what these imply. They need to be freed from the depressing sense of being just bewildered onlookers. As has been stated, their problem is not one of lacking intelligence, but of motion. Much depends on our not misconceiving their situation by considering them stupid because they react so poorly and do not seem to grasp situations and ideas. What they lack, in the widest sense, is a capacity to experience processes, deeper connections between things that are going on or being talked about. In other words, they cannot move inwardly with the motion taking place in their environment.

They are helped by being involved in easily understood series of practical actions or simple steps in doing or creating something, getting them first to take on one particular step in the production while merely observing what preceded and what follows it. The next time they take another step, and on each further occasion another, until all the steps have been accomplished. After that, the child is given command of a team of, say, mother and father, telling them what their job is while choosing for herself the part she wants to assume.

Baking and cooking are examples of suitable activities. And when the children are a little older, they can help prepare wool for knitting and weaving, washing, combing, dyeing and spinning. Social games can be played, making up stories where the child can contribute simple bits of dialogue. Still later, stories can be made up that continue on from day to day, maintaining strict consistency in characterization, so that a good king does not do something bad, or penniless people suddenly take off on expensive travels.

Another very rewarding procedure is to go for a walk with the child every week, at the same time, on the same day, or the same walk always stopping at the same places—a tree, a garden fence, a building site—and with the child ascertaining what has changed or not changed. They should describe in detail alterations to the building, the flowers that have blossomed, and those that have already wilted, the leaves of tree that have changed color, and so on. Week by week every change is noted and discussed with the child, as in a ritual. And if, as can easily happen, some of the same people are encountered, their same or changed activities can be made themes of ongoing speculative stories about them.

Such devices encourage participating with lively attention and fantasy in the world process. Depressed, brooding children are greatly helped thereby. The term "world process" used here is not to be taken as meaning anything lofty or grandiose. It refers to concrete, everyday physical experiences such as can provide stimulation for the inner compositor.

What obviously has therapeutic effect on such children is, for one thing, learning to take playful part in social processes that follow certain matter-of-course rules of listening and replaying, of exchanging roles, of reacting with presence of mind to what one's companion does.

But caution is needed here, for depressed, brooding children find games of this kind very difficult. Therefore, too much should not be expected of them, as that would result in the opposite of what we want to achieve. These children need careful involvement, and guidance, carried out with real understanding of their weak points. "Involvement" is the key word in dealing with them.

The second thing to consider is, as already mentioned, everything that has to do with playing parts, with games involving gesture, and dancing, all imitative activity and movement dialogue. These are purest therapy for the souls of depressed children, provided the situations are not too demanding and that trusted guidance is available for them to fall back on in case of need.

FORMED SPEECH: MEANINGFUL GESTURE

Speech and conversing are both important and need to receive attention. The best therapist is a person trained in speech formation and used to working with children. Such an individual's contribution may be likened to that of a curative eurythmist. And provision should be made at home for someone available to hold conversations with the child as often as possible, to explain what needs explaining and to unravel meaning, so that the child does not have a chance to brood. Conversations with very young children are, of course, exercises in image-making, in presenting the world in pictures rather than in abstract terminology.

That holds true with children of school age as well, though conversations can advance to pointing out and discussing things to notice, like phenomena, or to a description of how people react to this and that, how they feel, what they are afraid of, their temperaments and peculiarities.

Our own way of speaking is by no means a matter of small consequence. In the presence of depressed, brooding children we should take special trouble to speak beautifully and musically. I do not mean artificially—anything but!—just clearly and distinctly, so that the child notices the controlled will in our speech, the element of freedom. (Quite aside from its pedagogical significance, clear, free, conscious speech is well worth acquiring.)

It is very good for depressed children to engage in lots of reciting of poetry and in singing.

What applies to the speaking of sounds applies also to expressive body speech or movement. We should pay attention in our daily life with all children, but especially with depressed ones, to the way we move. Is there still a trace of musicality, or life, still left from the time when we were involved in sports or enjoyed dancing, a remnant of the natural grace that goes with being young? We work in a healthy way on the imitative nature of every child who witnesses beauty in the speech of our gestures and bodily motion. Beauty comes into being when we participate in life in a fluid and farsighted way, just by taking time and approaching the most ordinary, practical matters with inner participation. That lends a certain aesthetic note to our movement which children, and the little ones especially, perceive and unconsciously imitate as a confidence-inspiring element. We must not forget that the "milieu" of the sense of motion is consciously formed movement, meaningful gesture.

As we saw earlier in our study, children respond in their tendency to imitate the good and to the bodily experience we give them of being loved. That depends in the first place, on bodily contact that fosters the life-and touch senses and springs from a reverential approach and basic consideration and participatory interest. But the way we behave around a child, the way we deal with things and with others, our interrelating, is of great importance. Take, for example, whether we pay attention to a child in the room with us, or occupy ourselves with something else. Our way of relating, our inner attitude, expresses itself in the speaking way we move, and children's sense of their own motion "speaks" inwardly accompanying it.

We need not concern ourselves, at this point, with the details of how this accompanying, "inner speaking" functions. All we need to know is that young children are fractionally involved in it and move in a way that affects their overall sensing of vitality as well as the fact that the sense of motion is also drawn in and works upon their soul development.

So let us pay attention to the language of gesture! I repeat that it is not a question of practicing in front of a mirror, but of attitude. What we do lovingly is done automatically, in the sense of unconsciously, in such a manner that a child is satisfied in his sense of motion's expectations.

EDUCATION AND SELF-EDUCATION: COMPASSIONATE CAPACITY

Here again we can build on the angel's activity, which, in relation to the sense of motion, can be described as relaxing, coordinating support. During the night, the whole system of limbs and muscles is as though revised. Tensions are relaxed, and the musculature devotes itself to serving a quiet, even flowing of body fluids. We surrender our bodies completely to gravity; we also escape its clutches, since we no longer need to oppose it. Our higher components free themselves from our bodies and are suffused by supersensory forces, which enable us, in the movement of standing and walking, to make use of that miraculous system of our muscular structure and coordination, operating, at every movement, below the level of consciousness.

The angel works relaxingly, relieving tension, like an extraordinarily sensitive, adept masseur, taking the exhausted inner composer under its inspiring and regenerating care. When, upon awakening, this inner composer resumes its work, it finds the body that is its instrument supple and tractable, able to take up its activities newly strengthened.

This should not be taken as poetic allegory. The subject matter is obviously conducive to speaking in images. But they are images that describe actual happenings, although we have no accustomed words for them.

What do we think enables a newborn infant to acquire, within a short period, the capacity to stand upright, to walk, to learn to talk? By imitating, certainly. But who, after listening to a Beethoven sonata, can sit down at the piano and say that he has learned by imitation to play the sonata? Before that happens we have to learn to play the piano. Otherwise, we would not have to begin with the sonata. Where it is a matter of imitation, children have obviously learned to play the piano before birth; we do not need to teach it to them. They are scarcely born before, of their own accord, they are "practicing the most difficult pieces," and there is nothing in the educational line that we have to do, either to motivate them or to show them how it is done. They know perfectly what to do in order, at ten or eleven months, to be able to stand upright and walk about like grownups. All we have to do is to move about upright where they can see us.

Would we be able, in a year's time, to play the Beethoven sonata after listening to someone else playing it during that period? No! That would not be of the best use if we did not know how pianos are played.

So why does a child learn to walk from seeing us do it? Why, because she can imitate. That remarkable skill, at which the child is adept right from the start, was taught her by her angels.

That a higher wisdom is at work in children must be apparent to unprejudiced observers. It works in a variety of ways. And as regards their inborn (but as yet immature) mobile intelligence, we can say—to express it in a short formula—that the same wisdom that sees to their being born as imitators provides in every night of sleep, a freeing-coordinating refurbishing of their whole structural makeup. This makes it possible for the sense of motion to undergo gradual development and to take over that sense's basic orientating function. In the angels' freeing-coordinating action, children have a deep unconscious experience of the quality of sensitive understanding that can be raised to the level of love, and they turn to the world and to their fellow human beings with longing expectation of again encountering that same sensitivity.

We fulfill this expectation when we respond with the corresponding positive attitude to children's imitative feeling for meaningful, "beautiful" movement and reassure them that they will never be left uncaringly to their own devices, but rather always included in what is happening. They experience joy in living when we treat them with the sympathy that is "understanding raised to the level of the force of love" in social life. This strengthens "the sense of oneself as a free soul" and lays the foundation for the child's later discovering in himself a matter-of-course capacity for compassion. Sermons about kindness and mercifulness do not bear educational fruit, but educational deeds that nurture the sense of motion do. Depressed, brooding children have a particular need of just such support. And they need, more than other children, a sense feeling of being understandingly included, since exclusion from what goes on around them is their worst trauma.

Their dilemma might be compared to that of a musician who comes well prepared to an orchestra rehearsal, but breaks down every time, because he is so upset by the multiplicity of sounds around him that he just sits there as though paralyzed and prefers not playing at all to continually playing wrong.

That is about the situation in which a child with an inadequately developed sense of motion finds himself as he comes through the kindergarten door every morning. He is unable to coordinate, in his own being, all the things going on around him. He lacks inner adjustability, a proper mixture of ease and instinctive situation sense. These children, therefore, always seem to themselves to be "sand in the gearbox." So they stay out of things as far as possible. The compulsiveness we sometimes note in them has the characteristics of a ritual. They create their own meaningful world by setting up orderly systems of procedure within which every detail has its understood ritualistic place and significance.

These are the aspects of the depressed, brooding nature that I wanted to bring to your attention. Children with these traits have not been significantly permeated, in the way they feel and in their relationship with others, by the freeing and coordinating activity of their angels. What is given them in sleep is not enough to counter the stormy world of the senses. That is what makes them want to withdraw into themselves, as though seeking connection with the realm from which security and harmony flow as they close the gates to the outer world.

THE SENSE OF BALANCE

It is obvious that the sense of balance is closely related to the sense of motion. Our whole feeling of being at ease, our whole capacity for coordination, would be as good as useless if we were unable to keep our balance. In every sequence of movements, in every moment of just standing upright, balance has to be continuously maintained. The sense of balance plays a basic role in the fine tuning of our muscles, and the complementary equalizing impulses and "compositioning" accomplishments of the feeling realm that have been a subject of discussion here would not be possible without a subtle capacity for perceiving balance and imbalance.

Despite this, however, the sense of balance has a unique quality not shared by the sense of motion. Rudolf Steiner describes it as follows: "What is our perception of the experience rayed into the soul by the sense of balance? It is wholly of a soul nature. We perceive it as inner quiet, inner quiet of such a kind that if I walk from here to there I don't leave behind what is occupying my body; I take it along with me. And it remains its own same quiet self. Even if I were to take to the air and fly, it would remain as it was. And that is what makes us independent of time. I don't leave myself behind going from today to tomorrow; I stay the same. This independence of time comes from the raying into the soul of the sense of balance. It is a sensing of oneself as spirit."

This is an unaccustomed view at first glance! We usually start out with the crude premise that because we have a sense of balance, we do not fall over!

And quite right, too! Rudolf Steiner often spoke of this salient aspect of it, as when he referred to "the sense that enables us to distinguish whether we're standing up or lying down, and to perceive how we keep balanced standing on our two legs." More exact scrutiny leads to questioning whether it isn't absolutely astounding that we can keep our balance while standing still. We take it as a perfectly normal fact, and it is that, of course, but even so, miraculous.

Think what an enormously disproportionate weight is carried on the minimal surface of the soles of our feet, as though that were nothing to wonder at! And these soles do that carrying not only when we are standing as straight as tin soldiers, but when we are dancing or hopping on one leg. I weigh 210 pounds and can, nevertheless, assure you that I neither feel heavy nor am in any danger of toppling over, provided I do not engage in any crazy gyrations. I can indeed hop on one leg, in spite of my weight, and even keep my balance when walking on a fence. One notices how amazing it is to carry a lot of weight around without feeling heavy when, for some reason, say after riding on a merry-go-round, or drinking alcohol, one's balance is thrown out of kilter. On such occasions, one has to navigate carefully and, above all, not close one's eyes.

The sense of sight is handed an important equalizing function when the sense of balance is thrown out. We cling to objects with our eyes, seeking inner orientation in external spatial situations. If festive celebrations have not reached a point affecting our sight, we are able to correct an uncertain balance by keeping our eyes open. If we close them, matters can become critical. If we lean over backwards to study the sky, the same is true, or if we whirl around too fast.

What is happening in such cases?

The phenomenon is that of a disturbed internal, spatial orientation. We have an internal sensing of space that is not identical with external, spatial perception, and it is normally present even when we close our eyes and stuff up our ears. It might be called, more precisely, an inner sensing of symmetry. We have an inner experience of how we are related to the spatial directions up/down, right/left, front/back. These are purely inner experiences of space, quite distinct from those of external spaces. We sense ourselves in them as upright, erect forms standing within an inner space, as vertical figures at space's very center. There is always an experience of being at a middle point when we stand and concentrate on our inner sense of spatial orientation, the experience of a midpoint and of upward extension. Space extends, cupola-like, evenly, in all directions, and at its center stands the ego, erect. This fundamental sensing of symmetry is always there, beneath the surface, whenever we are in a state of balance. That is what Rudolf Steiner meant when he talked of "an inner quietness that makes us seem independent" of time and embodiment.

Our above-described, inner perception of balance does, however, have some relationship with our bodily condition in that it is involved in the totality of our makeup as human beings; we saw this in discussions of its connection with the other senses, of the way our soul-spiritual nature relates to the physical body. But the aspect of that relationship conveyed to us by the sense of balance is that of the independence of the former from the latter. For the physical body, left to itself, is subject to gravity. It is exposed to centrifugal forces that pull it down towards the earth's center. If we were fully controlled by it we would not be able to stand upright or to walk but only would be able to creep at best. But even creeping demands some degree of independence from the law of gravity, for where nothing exists to counter gravitation, there is no such countering at all; there is no mobility whatsoever, no self-moving bodies.

We can judge from the fact that not even night crawlers or worms are totally subject to their physical bodies to the astounding degree human beings have emancipated themselves in the course of their development as souls and spirits. There are physical laws to which human beings would have been fully subjected if there were no souls and egos in their bodies to enable them to stand upright and to move. Walking and standing, we have an experience of our emancipation. And we have no sense of being pulled down, of heaviness, when we dance, or hop on one foot, or balance on a fence. We could not do any of these things without that sensing of inner symmetry and space, of being "up-borne in our soul-space," of "being spirits," as Rudolf Steiner described it. A flower, we learn, is drawn upward by sunlight. It grows upwards and opens because the sun shines. We human beings have within us light that enables us to erect and open ourselves to what lies above. That is what the sense of balance makes possible for us to perceive: that inner light, lifting us erect and opening us to the sphere where angels dwell.

Freeing arms and hands

The sense of motion enables us to experience mobility (dynamics) within our soul space, while the sense of balance transmits a sensing of our inner-space, or soul space, as such. The above-described experiencing of erectness in the center of our spatial placement is the basic experience of symmetry (statics). Thus, these two senses work together conveying information as to our soul-spiritual condition as it relates to the body physical, and also to its relationship to what surrounds us. We are bodily-physically involved in that relationship, and thereby subject to the physical laws of our surroundings. As soul-spiritual beings we perceive the manner and extent of that involvement, as well as the extent of our partial noninvolvement, by means of our basal senses.

It is the sense of motion that gives us an absolutely clear sensing, in the form of "the experience of being free souls," of our partial freedom from subjection to bodily-physical determinants. But at the same time, the perception we have of the dynamics taking place around us is a very marked one. The sensing of free mobility in our soul-space originates in a living interchange with "the moved and moving action going on in the world" in decidedly time-related experiences. Nevertheless, an essence of our relationship with our surroundings survives, transcending time and place, and gradually becomes a lasting soul possession.

The case of the sense of balance is a different one. It gives us a far clearer perception than the sense of motion does of being lifted above the bodily level of experience; we sense it as an erective capacity, as weightlessness. It is not by chance that Rudolf Steiner says, "I could fly through the air and remain quietly the same." The experience is one of a time-related erectness in the soul area, such that Rudolf Steiner says of it," It is wholly a soul experience, perceived as inner quiet." Our ability to move freely is the product of the soul. The soul moves in the space created by the interplay between gravity working downward and our ego force working upward.

Closer observation reveals that the sensing of freedom of movement originates in the fact that our soul element interacts with our vital life processes, while the sensing of oneself as spirit is the product of the ego's activity in the physical body.

However, we do not need to pursue study of the human entelechy very far to understand how this applies to children. Rudolf Steiner discussed this in Lecture 2 of his book, *The Child's Changing Consciousness as the Basis of Pedagogical Practice*, Apr. 15-22, 1923. I will quote him here at greater length. He says,

> You see "walking" is a term that actually covers more than is popularly thought. It covers a great deal more than just the fact that a child goes on from crawling to the upright walking that he will be doing for the rest of his life. Learning to walk means adjusting oneself or orientating oneself in such a manner that the entire balance of one's organism and all one's mobile possibilities insert themselves into the ordered balance and mobile possibilities of the universe, to the limit of

human inclusion in it. As we learn to walk, we are seeking this adjustment. We search for the unique relationships, occurring in human beings only, between the movement of our arms and hands and the movement of the other limbs. The arms and hands are assigned to the life of the soul, while the legs go on serving bodily movement. This is of immense importance for all later life—the differentiating between the two kinds of movement is a search for lifelong soul balance. We first seek physical balance in standing erect, but we seek soul-balance in freeing arm and hand mobility. We ought really to say that learning to walk is learning the statistics and dynamics of our own inner being as these are related to the universe, and that then, later on, in acquiring these skills, we absorb the spirit from our surroundings.

We see here again that we have a well-oriented sense of balance when the relationship between the upper and the lower human being is in a certain right adjustment. This provides, on the one hand, for the possession of a feeling of free inner mobility, and on the other, for a timeless sense of inclusion in the symmetry of the universe. Light's erective power lays hold on the physical body (the legs and feet) as a static force and forces the dynamic capacity of the arms and hands, enabling us to insert our upper limbs into the movement patterns of the cosmos. The combination of the two allows us to experience the statics of our "mid-point erectness" and "space-vanquishing" dynamics. The former is the product of the lower limbs, the latter of the upper, breast-centered ones.

It is only as a result of the higher limbs lifting themselves above the realm of the lower, earthbound limbs that we can partake of the feeling of being free souls that has been described as based on the sense of motion. The balance-derived rulership of the arms and hands makes itself felt as an experiencing of the above-mentioned capacity, which combines the perception of oneself in movement, transmitted by the sense of motion, with perception of the adjusting and coordinating ability referred to as free relatedness to the cosmic order.

Judgement and the sense of balance

We see here again how the senses of balance and motion interpenetrate one another. Soul balance rests upon the fact that the upper human is both anchored by and lifted above the lower one, suffusing but not absorbed into it. The upper human brings the lower human into upright stance and grows beyond it. "We seek physical balance in our uprightness. But soul balance is sought in the freeing of our arms and hands." The spirit "taken into us in the process," as Rudolf Steiner puts it, is received as a gift of the angel's activity. Angels are, so to speak, the transmitters from whom "balance and the possibilities of cosmic movement" ray into us. Again, this happens at night when the higher components of the human makeup ("the ego and the astral body," as they are called in anthroposophical terminology) release themselves from physical-bodily bonds and "load up" the forces needed upon awakening for standing up again and walking.

Rudolf Steiner's use of terms borrowed from physics to illustrate these connections emboldens me to speak of loading up here. But the "statics" of human balance is obviously not the same as that operative in, say, a building, for that would mean either sacrificing our free mobility or getting blown over by every puff of wind. The ego and astral body are certainly not loaded up with forces like batteries being charged with electricity. What actually happens is that youngsters are being taught while they sleep (and grown-ups, too, though theirs is a diminished dependence).

They are being taught how to achieve free mobility in a proper alteration of freeing (loosening), relaxing, and coordinating movement. They are taught how to harmonize statics and dynamics in a relationship balanced between gravity (groundedness) and levity (emancipation of the upper limbs) in the process of achieving upright posture. Such are the lessons taught by angels on the score of the sense of motion and sense of balance complex.

By means of these senses, and in carrying over what we learn in sleep to our daytime experience, we perceive ourselves and the world around us. We owe it to the instruction received in sleep that we are able, when awake, not only to stand upright but also to go on absorbing the spirituality that holds sway around about us, organizing the material-spatial world. What physics, mathematics, and astronomy describe (not their speculations, but what they discover as law-abiding fact in the course of thoughtful observation) are actually universal divine principles which, if we lacked the sense of balance, we would have no capacity to understand. Without that sense we would experience the spatial world and its content as a conglomeration of unrelated objects, processes, and conditions rather than as an ordered structure. To put it another way, we would be unable to think clearly if we possessed no sense of balance.

"If we didn't have a sense that enabled us to keep in balance while standing still, moving and dancing, it would be impossible to achieve full consciousness," says Rudolf Steiner.

In a nutshell, if we are dizzy we have no perspective, no grasp of things. The exact sciences would never have come into being without the sense of balance. We couldn't have acquired the power of judgment that comes to expression archetypally in "the freed activity of the arms and hands." This activity is a primal phenomenon, the development of which is seen in the polarity between levity and gravity, vertically and horizontally. Adequate orientation in the matter of balance resolves any question as to what is up and what is down, what is vertical and what is horizontal (and even with what is here and what is there, although the differentiating aspect of the sense of touch also plays a role here).

Thomas Göbel writes in his *Sources of Art* that "the absolute nature of the spirit is seen again in the phenomena of the sense that serves the spirit." The perceptions conveyed by the sense of balance invariably have but a single meaning. No such thing as a mixture of phenomena ever occurs.

Our arms and hands "weigh" everything they pick up. Or, to express it more accurately, what lives in them when they are not involved in some physical activity is the inner "weighing" that we carry out with our powers of judgment. We see this in the instinctive weighing motions that we make with our hands and arms when we feel ambivalent or are uncertain about a decision.

This weighing is a wholly automatic act that brings a highly significant aspect of our sensing of balance to expression. Why do we feel the need to decide between opposites rather than just let them be? Making judgments means arriving at an outlook that resolves or rises above a problem, a process in which what at first seems insoluble is brought into harmonious accord.

This need that we feel originates in our constant striving to create balance. We sense that we are not in balance when we are confronted by an unsolved contradiction or a crass one-sidedness. So we try to restore symmetry in our thinking and feeling. In such situations we try instinctively to restore ourselves inwardly to an erect stance, one from which we can gain an overview and create an order in harmony with the balance and lawful movement of the cosmos, the divine world order.

Rather than discussing the moral world order and the role that freedom plays in it, I will simply call attention here to the fact that right and wrong reveal traces of synchronism and anachronism. These traces are summed up in the term "sense of justice." The sense of justice is simply a sublimation of the sense of balance coupled with the capacity for empathy transmitted by the sense of motion. Fellow feeling and compassion are indissolubly bound up, though not identical, with the sense of justice. Far from a moral standpoint, a feeling for justice is feeling for symmetry, an inner impulse to bring restitution in restoring human dignity where it has suffered.

Empathy is what is needed in such cases, to avoid resorting to rigid theoretical principles. Let me remind you here that since Christ, justice without empathy has not been held an acceptable principle. But empathy alone is not enough. What is needed is an empathy-permeated capacity to grasp what on a moral level is "a balanced human relationship to the cosmos."

And that is the direction in which we are working when we nurture a child's senses of balance and motion. We lay the foundation for lifelong soul balance when we help children to free their arms and hands, and indeed their whole breast area, from the pull of gravity, working to assist their angel to develop in them a sure sense and respect for human dignity in the form of the sense of justice. A capacity for compassion and the sense of justice are the two moral-social capacities related to the motion- and balance-sense complex, just as tolerance and caring are related to the life- and touch-sense complex.

We note, as we survey all this, that these are the four aspects to what the Christian ideal resolves into one and calls love of one's neighbor.

Now someone might object, "Isn't it materialistic thinking to dismiss the lofty nature of the sense of justice as just a sublimated feeling for symmetry?"

Anyone making such an objection might think back to our initial agreement to avoid such misunderstandings by adhering to a certain way of viewing things. "Moral discernment may be the final product of an evolutionary process, but nevertheless as an inner motive it is, by our definition of 'moral,' always primary, never secondary."

That is what we are concerned with here. The lightening (erecting), integrating (unifying) support given by children's angels to their sense of balance (i.e., to their feeling for space and symmetry) is an endowment in the form of moral discernment. A developed sense of balance is synonymous with imitative readiness to uphold everything that satisfies one's sense of justice.

Children experience their angels' lightening and integrating support in deep unconsciousness as incitement to develop their ability to pass judgment into a capacity for love, that is, into a higher sense of justice. This causes them to long for, and to expect to find, this quality in the way we adults live and relate to our fellow human beings. If the ideal of justice is alive within us, not just as a mental concept but as a genuine social impulse, it will have an orienting effect on children's sense of balance. Just as we have to develop patience in order to become tolerant, just as we have to be interested participants to feel caring, just as we have to be inwardly mobile to experience compassion, so the sense of justice requires a certain measure of balanced judgment, a certain equanimity that transcends the calm state of soul transmitted by the life sense.

The equanimity that is the outgrowth of the sense of balance is characterized above all by openness and relatedness. Feeling for space and symmetry develops of itself in grownups; children at first do not possess it. It originates in our attaining spatial balance and a relationship to gravity by our own efforts, as Rudolf Steiner emphasizes. And Schenrle writes that, "the correspondence between our own body weight and the surrounding world is perfect. It is in just this fact that the indissoluble unity of the world and the self becomes physically visible." Equanimity or soul balance is also a quality that reveals itself only in relationship to our surroundings and our fellow human beings. It finds behavioral expression in farsightedness, in sureness as we make decisions and arrive at judgments, in calm pursuit of one's goals, in a sense of order (though not in that compulsive orderliness that indicates an actual lack of inner balance), and in an ability to see situations in their wholeness.

What radiates from individuals with good inner balance is something uncommonly confidence inspiring. It has a direct stabilizing effect on a child's balance, not just on soul balance but on his bodily balance as well.

I am only too aware of the difficulties this presents. But if we are to be capable of wholesome, constructive self-criticism, we have to know what is called for. Where the development of a child's sense of balance is concerned, we ought not to entertain any illusions about the effect our own soul balance has on the child's, but rather ask ourselves how believable or unbelievable, reliable or unreliable, we are in matters involving right and wrong. Preaching justice is ineffective; only one's own effort to be absolutely straight in moral issues, to be guided by what we feel is right—a sense we all possess—will do.

Rarely, we lack this sense. The problem is rather that we are often tempted to disregard it, to pay no attention to the prompting of the voice of conscience, in fact even to feel it as bothersome.

No, we don't need to be superheroes to be good parents—nothing of the sort! If one plays that lofty, deceitful role with children, they withdraw into themselves in distrust, for they are well aware what is genuine and what is false. Young children, unlike adults, are not interested in results, in products. What they notice is the honest effort. As Schenrle says, "The symbol of balance, the scale, is the age-old symbol of justice."

In parental striving in this direction, in nurturing a certain soul discipline, dealing justly with our children, always concerned to be fair and unprejudiced in relationships with others, we nourish a child's sense of balance. That is moral education for the future! We cannot expect small children to have a feeling for justice; that lies deep in their unconsciousness as their angels' message, "working" from the night side on children's balance structure. But we can count on their imitative readiness to absorb everything that finds expression in our own love-enhanced sure judgment, in our own sense of justice. Working in this way by day, we support children's discovery of their own balance, and later on their entirely matter-of-fact discovery of a sense of justice of their own.

THE GIFT OF WALKING:
THE LEADING ROLE PLAYED BY THE SENSE OF BALANCE

My experience has not led to distinguishing a definite type of child with a disturbed sense of balance, as it has done in the case of the other senses. It is clear that depressed, brooding children will suffer poor balance orientation in addition to the disturbed sense of motion typical of them. But children of the restless-nervous and anxious-timid types can also not be expected to exhibit soul balance.

Our contemplation of the sense of balance shows it to be that sense whereby the angel's presence and activity in a child's body-soul makeup are most observable. Ordering and harmonizing, shaping and configuring, loosening and consolidating—these functions are various aspects of a single higher lightening and integrating formative power that governs the incarnation process and lays the foundation for soul-balance in our lives. When children begin to refer to themselves as "I" (around their third year), they have completed the first stage of the maturing of the sense of balance; we see that the hidden force at work in the development of the life sense and the senses of touch and motion is now revealing itself in its true nature.

Karl König, that great pioneer in the field of therapeutic sense doctrine, wrote in his book, *The Child's First Three Years*, that with the attainment of balance the head lifts up into the light. The antithesis between gravity and levity is achieved and imaged in the (new) upright posture. This new development cannot be looked upon in any other way than as connected with that member of the human entelechy called by Rudolf Steiner "the ego," possessed by human beings alone of all the earth's creatures. It is the ego that enables every human being to become a partaker of the divine gift of walking. All the other forms of movement subordinate themselves to the single figure, which (walking) makes the impression of an upright energy, and in the act of walking takes over the coordinating and directing of the whole complex.

This divine gift is brought by the child from the angel sphere at birth. And the child returns nightly to that sphere to make sure of his possession.

As regards its connection with the other basal senses, it is obvious that the dynamic self-perception afforded by the life sense and the sense of touch would have no significance whatsoever for the development of consciousness, if the perceiver were not erect and perceiving her own uprightness. Schenrle terms the sense of balance "the top coordinator of the somatic sphere," and shows that "moving, touching, and the vital sensations derived from a state of well-being by which we become conscious of our bodies are invariably linked in the last analysis to our specific sensing of symmetry and inner direction." Summing up, we can say with Göbel that "the sense of balance provides the gate through which the ego passes to experience its twenty-four-hour rhythm, alternating between waking bodily awareness and withdrawal from that awareness in sleep."

In addition to paying attention to our educational attitudes and to our overall stance in life, we further a child's sense of balance by taking into account everything that has significance in nurturing the other bodily senses, particularly the sense of motion. A latent weakness of the sense of balance always accompanies weakening of the whole spectrum of the lower senses, where, it should be noted, the real cause of difficulty lies. If a small child fails to be properly imitative and turns in upon herself, special attention should be paid to her sense of motion. If, on the other hand, an unnatural going-along-with-everything takes the place of healthy, creative imitating, persisting perhaps to the age of five or six without any interludes of rebellion, so that by school age the child is being unresistingly carried along with whatever goes on around her, then the sense of touch requires special attention. Thirdly, if the imitative urge is present but always being interrupted by darts into restlessness and convulsive movement, if we observe that this unrest is in response to impressions from outside that seem to be attacking the child and causing her to keep up constant body-soul resistance and constant counter motion—whether it be against food, optical, or acoustic disturbances—then the child's sense of motion needs looking at, as well as the touch sense, but the primary cause is a disturbance of the life with every experience of touch sense.

In all these cases, cited only as examples, there is some degree of involvement of the sense of balance. And when we see that its lack of development is the major problem, when a child does not begin to straighten up properly, and even has trouble standing and walking, in spite of growing up in caring circumstances where neglect and mistreatment cannot be held accountable, the cause usually lies in a defect of the central nervous system. From the anthroposphical viewpoint, this would be looked upon as a partial impermeability of the bodily instrument whose function it is to serve the higher members of our makeup. The pedagogical therapy in such a case would include all four of the lower senses in therapeutic developmental exercises such as Dieter Schulz has described in a book earlier referred to.

SOUL BALANCE AND SELF-ESTEEM

Every difficulty experienced by a child in the incarnation process has its effect on the sense of balance. It is, therefore, not as easy to outline a type in the case of children with obvious impairment of that sense as it is in cases of impairment of the primary senses: the life sense and the senses of touch and motion. We can ask, however, what characterizes a deficiency of soul balance when it crops up in relationship to basic problems of the other three senses.

Here we must focus our attention on the erective process that Karl König had in mind when he wrote, "the head lifts, reaching toward the light." This is a highly significant statement about the self-perception, the self-valuing that play such a role today! What modern psychological jargon describes in these terms (and in the motto, "Tell yourself a hundred times a day how terrific you are," which tends to glorify rather than really strengthen) is the sensing of oneself as spirit, called by Rudolf Steiner, "the raying up into the soul sphere of the sense of balance."

Restless-nervous, anxious-timid, and depressed-moody children all share damaged self-esteem, each type in its own characteristic way.

Let us recall these ways. The first feels himself unappreciated; the second, left to his own devices; the third, rejected and misunderstood. All are ways expressive of a lack of inner balance. And all the children suffering them go through life finding it hard to lift their heads. It must, therefore, be our finest striving to help them by giving them every reason to feel that they can connect to our tolerant appreciation, our interested participation, our complete and empathetic understanding.

A sense of self-esteem as a feeling of being lifted into the light and shone through is identical with experiencing freedom in the use of hands and arms. Here, too, all children who suffer weak orientation in the area of the bodily senses are vulnerable. They lack confidence in handling themselves, some as the result of restlessness, some from timidity, some from problems of understanding. All feel in common that they are failures. We must lift off this burden by helping them to gain confidence in the formative power of their hands as the first step in self-valuing. That is the basic pedagogical motif for the sense of balance and thus for overcoming all the orientational weaknesses from which the bodily senses suffer.

Consequently, the very worst mistake an educator can make is the unfortunately widespread habit of confronting the children, upset by a sense of failure, with their inadequacy. While their small successes should be given warm recognition, an unfinished or miscarried project brought by the child to the teacher should, without a lot of talk about it, be brought to a satisfying conclusion with praise at the end. This compassionate approach should be the prevailing one all through children's schooling! It too often happens that an awkward, timid, or confused child is taken to task, in a moralizing tone, for being lazy or for being deliberately obstructive or ill-behaved.

There is no such thing as a deliberately mean, lazy, or rebellious child! Every one of them longs from the bottom of his heart to do well and to be praised for it. It is we who turn them into lazy bones and rebels by reproaching them in their need. What on earth is a typically depressed and moody child, one that suffers from confusion as to what is being asked of him, to do when he is constantly being called an ill-bred, inattentive lazybones, and the other children are forever being held up as shining examples?

The time comes when children in this category simply refuse, for their own protection, to cooperate. *If we were to make it a habit to recognize that every child has his own yardstick by which his accomplishments have to be measured, there would not only be far fewer clients for pediatric counselors but many fewer catastrophic lives lived.*

The careers of many a criminal, sociopath, and devotee of some sect or other start from wounds caused by a child's fear of parents' or teachers' impatience and lovelessness, wounds so continually reopened that they never heal. Schools are the worst sinners in this respect. My experience as a professional medical counselor forces me to admit with sorrow that Waldorf schools are not that much better than public schools in the matter of understanding treatment of children whose behavior shows them to belong to the three basic types we have been discussing here. The encouraging exceptions that stand out when we encounter exemplary teachers should be acknowledged, with the comment that they occur more frequently in Waldorf schools than elsewhere.

In any case, the problems of children who do not fit the norm is a sad story. They should not be attributed to any one teacher, but rather to the overall shortcomings of school systems (overcrowded classrooms, the need for special professional help, too little emphasis given to educational therapy in teacher training, insufficient qualitative standards in training courses, lack of freedom in dealing with curriculum, and so on.) These are some of the areas in which desperately needed solutions should be sought. For there will be more, rather than less, children in the future who will be in need of special help, but who neither could nor should be removed to special schools or homes, first, because they do not fit in such extreme categories, and, secondly, out of ordinary humane consideration.

To sum up, all schools will go in the direction of partially therapeutic institutions whether we want them to or not, and it would be an excellent thing for the Waldorf school movement if it were to stand shoulder-to-shoulder with therapists and supply innovative ideas for this inevitable development rather than lag behind.

Summary:

MEASURES FOR DEALING WITH DEPRESSED, BROODING CHILDREN

Let us review, in a comprehensive survey, the directional cues for educating depressed, brooding children, for nurturing the sense of motion- and-balance complex. We are dealing here, as we have seen, with situations in which the sense of balance plays the leading role in conjunction with all the lower senses, but especially in relationship to the sense of movement. As Göbel puts it, "Our sense of balance and motion are closely coordinated and work together. We should observe their cooperation in making necessary distinctions." That is what we have done here. The following are basic aspects:

- Imitation

- Calm, meaningful motion

- Free play of the arms and hands

- Involvement in dance-like movement

- Sensing of balance/symmetry/ space

- Formed speech/recitation/music

123

- Helping to clarify situations

- Setting up orderly practical assignments

- Consciously relating to everyday events

- Unsentimental empathy as the basic
  educational approach

- Compassion as the model attitude

These are the directions to take with children in whom lack of soul balance is related to latent weakness of the sense of motion.

Conclusion: education and ethics

Encouragement is the educational maxim for restless, anxious, and depressed children. It is our own living respect for human dignity which gives them security. Such are the qualities that must take the place of the manipulative "raising" of children according to destructive norms which play a major role in our modern society. Do those who lack the compassion-informed sense of justice to recognize the significance of living respect for human worth, and those who deny that a child's welfare is just as important as an adult's, have any right to judge educational matters? No one who disregards values like tolerance, caring, compassion, and justice will understand certain basic phenomena and facts of human soul life or be able to help in shaping a developmental psychology that transcends present materialistic one-sidedness, a psychology still quite in its infancy such as we have represented here. Children do not just educate themselves, as the antiauthoritarians insist, nor are they educated by us alone, as the determinists contend. Education is primarily the job of spiritual beings drawing upon heavenly sources. Parents, teachers, and therapists merely round out what the angels do.

Children really do have guardian angels, their higher selves, who not only stand by in extreme situations, but regularly every night help to strengthen and comfort them. Parents who make it a conscious practice to support the angels' work with their own efforts and take care not to allow the days to undermine what the nights build up give their children innermost encouragement.

These are ideas, not fantasies, that the science of education will have to be guided by in order to keep social life from falling into catastrophic disarray. The solution of the social question is found in homes and classrooms, nowhere else.

We should take this conviction to heart. The future of our children obliges us to concern ourselves in depth with the new spirituality which begins where a new humane orientation develops from reverence for the child. Let us not go on demanding narcissistically that children revere us, but rather arouse in ourselves reverence for them and for the world of angels that they manifest.

All else follows. It is not easy, but we can begin today, and every effort counts.